ARIZONA
JOURNEY GUIDE
A DRIVING & HIKING GUIDE TO RUINS, ROCK ART, FOSSILS & FORMATIONS

WRITTEN BY JON KRAMER AND JULIE MARTINEZ
ILLUSTRATIONS BY VERNON MORRIS

Adventure Publications
Cambridge, Minnesota

SPECIAL THANKS

Road trips are always fun, especially when you have a guide with a competent vehicle. Such was the case with my visit to Quartzsite where Bob Donato generously gave me an unforgettable desert tour in his Swiss Army truck (see Precautions/Roads). If you can't go to Australia yourself it's nice to have a friend who'll give you decent photos along with tall tales. Thanks to Bruce and Lois Erickson for the photos of lava tube caves from Down Under (see Lava River Cave). It may seem like it's always sunny in Tucson but every time I've been to Signal Hill it rained. So I am indebted to my sister Diane Meyer for her photos of the spot, although I did note it was cloudy during her visit, so I don't feel all that bad about my luck there.

Photo credits by photographer and page number:
Cover photos by Jon Kramer and Julie Martinez: Montezuma Castle (main photo), Sears Point petroglyph (left inset), Window Rock (middle inset), Tyrannosaurus Rex skull (right inset)
All photos are copyright Jon Kramer and Julie Martinez unless otherwise noted.
Suzanne Aldrich: 98 **Eric J. Anderson**: 60, 62 (both), 196, 224, 226 (both), 232 **Arizona State Parks Foundation**: 112, 114 (both), 115 (both) **Dave Baker**: 88 **John Carranza**: 89, 90 (both), 91 (both) **Graham Christensen**: 143 **Charles Cobeen**: 152, 157 (bottom) **Bruce and Lois Erickson**: 125 **Grand Canyon National Park**: 25 (both), 92, 96 (both), 97 (both) **Colossal Cave Mountain Park Research Library**: 64, 66 (both), 67 (both) **Meteor Crater, Northern Arizona, USA**: 140 **Suzanne Moody/National Park Service**: 54, 56 (both), 57 (right) **Diane Meyer**: 204, 206 **National Park Service Photo**: 186 **Charles Rand**: 130, 132 (both), 133 (both) **S. Cyd Read**: 100 **Redemptorist Renewal Center/Peter Tran**: 180 **Jeff Sorensen**: 227 (both) **J. Cowan Stark**: 30, 32 (both), 33 (both) **Vermilion Cliffs National Monument**: 242 **Ric Zimmerman**: 102 (both), 103 (both)

Artwork credits by artist and page number:
Julie Martinez: 11, 12, 14, 15, 82, 94 **Vernon Morris**: 43, 48, 53, 63 (both), 78, 95, 142, 160, 177, 179, 184, 198, 218, 230

Cover and book design by Jonathan Norberg

10 9 8 7 6

Arizona Journey Guide: A Driving & Hiking Guide to Ruins, Rock Art, Fossils & Formations
Copyright © 2007 by Jon Kramer, Julie Martinez and Vernon Morris
Published by Adventure Publications
An imprint of AdventureKEEN
310 Garfield Street South
Cambridge, Minnesota 55008
(800) 678-7006
www.adventurepublications.net
All rights reserved
Printed in China
ISBN 978-1-59193-140-9 (pbk.)

AUTHORS' DEDICATIONS

To my parents, who instilled in their children a passion for exploring nature and a thirst for high adventure; to my two brothers and sister, who continue to inspire and encourage me that way; and to my beautiful wife and fellow adventurer, Julie, whose love guides me and whose knowledge of nature astounds me.

–JON KRAMER

To my parents with gratitude for all their support as I traveled and explored the wilderness through my life and to my wonderful husband, traveling companion, and best friend, Jon.

–JULIE MARTINEZ

A special thanks to Naomi, Spence and Duane Morris, mother and brothers, for a lifetime of encouragement and just being there.

–VERN MORRIS

The authors would like to extend a very special thanks to all who treat the earth with the reverence and respect she deserves. The Great Spirit smiles with you in the sunrise.

TABLE OF CONTENTS

WELCOME TO ARIZONA

When someone mentions the Southwest we imagine cactus-studded deserts, craggy sandstone buttes and ancient ruins tucked away in hidden canyons. It's all true and no place conjures up such images more vividly than Arizona, a land of endless diversity, great natural beauty and, yes, a lot of cactus. The problem is one can hardly scratch the surface of all the fantastic natural wonders of Arizona in a guide such as this. There's just too much for words, no matter how long-winded we might be. The following entries, therefore, are necessarily brief summations designed to give you a realistic feel for what's out there. They are intended as a tool to help you in planning your own adventure, be it by foot, mule, bicycle, car, RV or your own private spaceship.

Let's be up front about this right now: we do not restrict our listings here to government-sponsored sites or strict nonprofit organizations. To be sure, some of the best natural wonders in Arizona are private property, not reliant on tax dollars or grants for support. Meteor Crater and Rock Art Ranch are two outstanding examples of what private organizations can do. Besides, the government doesn't own every-thing—at least not yet—and free enterprise has made up for what the government lacks in some places.

Our work has allowed us the opportunity to recognize and enjoy the splendor of Arizona's ancient natural beauty. We've been traipsing around the state for decades reveling in the incredible diversity of its natural wonders and having the time of our lives. Each time we come home we have more fantastic stories to share with our friends. They, on the other hand, are sick and tired of hearing about our adventures, having long since turned cactus-green with envy. So inevitably, we began guiding our friends and other people to exciting places we've been, getting them started on their own adventures. That, in essence, is what compelled us to write this guide. It's our way of sharing the natural world we have enjoyed so much. And it also helps in getting these people off our backs.

We hope you have as much fun as we've had exploring the many natural wonders of Arizona.

Keep in touch!

Jon, Julie, & Vern

KEEP IN TOUCH

A few years back (like about 20, but who's counting...) there was a fellow in Bisbee, Arizona, by the name of Walter Swan who, in the 1980s, opened a shop called The One Book Bookstore where he sold only one book—that's right, just one title—his self-published autobiography *Me and Henry*. Critics scoffed at such an idea but Walter was undeterred. He plastered the walls of his shop with thousands of letters from folks the world over who bought his book and wrote him about it. The overwhelming response so encouraged him that he published a sequel and—you guessed it!—opened another shop right next door. The name? The Other Book Bookstore, of course. Walter and his books became something of a local legend as word spread and sales took off. From his first book alone, he sold over 30,000 copies in less than 5 years! Sadly, Walter passed away in 1995 and the bookstores closed.

Despite that, we thought his story was pretty neat. So we want to encourage you to do something similar. Now that you've bought this book, why not write us and fill us in on your adventures. Did our little guide here reinvigorate the ho-hum life of you and your partner, instilling a thirst for adventure and thereby save your marriage? We hope so. Or did you end up stuck in the mud for three days because you didn't follow our advice to check locally about road conditions, and now you need someone to take it out on? Go ahead, sock it to us, we're grown-ups (sort of). We want to know about it all—the good, the bad and, most certainly, the ugly. Who knows, maybe we'll open a bookstore and paper our walls with your letters!

Contact us at: www.JourneyGuides.com

or, write us at:

Arizona Journey Guide
c/o Adventure Publications, Inc.
820 Cleveland Street South
Cambridge, MN 55008

USING THIS GUIDE

About the listings

The sites appear in the book in alphabetical order as indicated below.

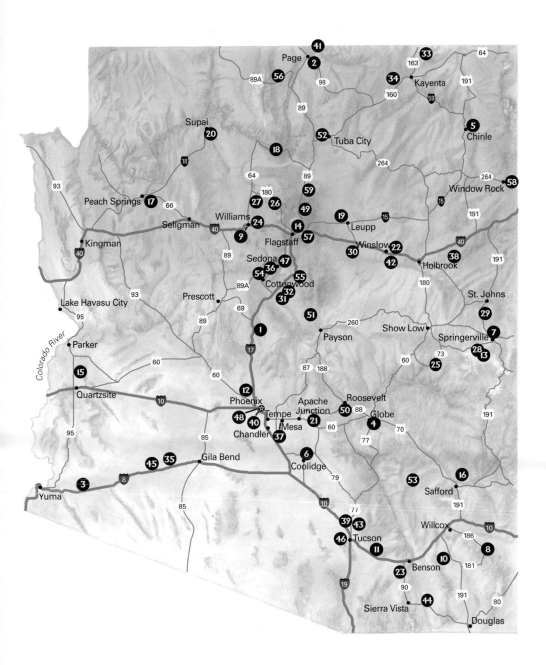

Page

Supai

Peach Springs

Seligman

Williams

Kingman

Flagstaff

Sedona

Prescott

Cottonwood

Lake Havasu City

Colorado River

Parker

Quartzsite

Phoenix

Tempe

Chandler

Mesa

Gila Bend

Coolidge

Yuma

Kayenta

Chinle

Window Rock

Tuba City

Leupp

Winslow

Holbrook

St. Johns

Springerville

Show Low

Payson

Apache Junction

Roosevelt

Globe

Safford

Willcox

Tucson

Benson

Sierra Vista

Douglas

Ratings

In the rating of each entry we give you an idea of the quality of experience you can expect with that aspect of the site. Our ratings are, admittedly, subjective. They are determined by our own personal standards. We take into account the quality and quantity of the subject matter, its educational value and presentation, and our overall impression of the experience visiting the site. We use a scale of 1–5 stars with an occasional half-star. Like in the hotel trade, five stars is top honors. Here's an approximation of how we rate things:

★☆☆☆☆: B-O-R-I-N-G and/or barely worthy of note, but for some reason we listed and rated it anyway.

★★☆☆☆: Stop by here if you're in the area and need to kill time. Who knows, you may like it more than the rating suggests.

★★★☆☆: Definitely worth a visit, no excuse necessary.

★★★★☆: This place warrants a detour and/or change of plans to visit, although you might want to stop short of divorcing your partner to get here.

★★★★★: Shazzam! This site is worthy of quitting your job and hitchhiking cross-country just to catch a glimpse of it. Go ahead, divorce your spouse if you need to—it's worth it!

After the ratings for each site, you'll note the category in parenthesis. This means that the site is rated in one or more of the following areas:

> archaeology
>
> geology
>
> paleontology
>
> museums

Therefore, the following entry would mean that this site is archaeologically significant, in Jon's opinion, but only mildly significant geologically.

Jon's Rating: ★★★★☆ (archaeology)

★☆☆☆☆ (geology)

★★★★☆ (museum)

Access

The ease with which you can access the main aspects of each location is indicated by a generalized rating. Remember, you are responsible for your own well-being. Things change all the time, especially in the no man's land of some of these places. Check beforehand with local land managers if you have any question about the difficulty. (By the way, we've included contact information so you can't whine about not knowing who to call for a road condition report.) In some cases, we indicate the difficulty of access by car to the trail head versus the difficulty of the trail itself. Trail access is loosely defined along these lines:

Easy
No real problem. The site is adjacent to parking or within a short, easy walk. If there are any complaints you've taken the wrong path.

Moderate
Usually requires some hiking over moderate topographic relief. No need for swearing and little-to-no sweat.

Difficult
Prolonged and/or rough hiking over significant topographic relief. There's likely to be some sweating here and the trek may occasionally warrant foul language.

Extreme
Very difficult, often multi-day hiking through rugged, remote terrain. Use of foul language and inappropriate gestures probable. Requires profuse sweating under arduous circumstances. Use deodorant.

Many places have multiple sites, some easy to access and others downright extreme. Such places will have a range of ratings that apply. For instance, the Grand Canyon has an Access rating of Easy to Extreme. A car or bus tour of the rim is easy. If, however, you wish to hike to Phantom Ranch at the bottom, then you're in for a very challenging, long trek that will test your fitness and likely your patience, thus warranting an "Extreme" rating.

Museums

 We've made a noble effort to inform you of all the natural history museums in the state. Keep in mind we do not list every museum in Arizona. We have not, for example, included the Titan Missile Museum or the Bead Museum, simply because they are not applicable to the type of journey you are reading about here. The museums we do include are notable educational institutions related to our listings in Archaeology, Paleontology and Geology. Besides being included in the site rating scales, these museums are listed on page 256.

INTRODUCING ARIZONA

Archaeology

 We came, we saw and we loved every minute of it. The result herein is a fairly comprehensive listing of all the publicly accessible archaeology sites in the state at the time of printing. We don't, however, attempt to document every single site you might be able to visit had you three weeks, Ironman endurance and a tanker-load of water. After all, the vast majority of Arizona archaeology sites have yet to be documented and many of these are on public land. But we do list those that a normal everyday traveler can access generally in one day with reasonable effort in decent weather.

We will not attempt to educate you on all the ins and outs of the various waves of human influence, occupation and cultures that play a role in the natural history of Arizona. Suffice to say, the list is long and very diverse, as you can see in the chart on the next page. The archaeology here is in a constant state of revision, with new sites and new theories being discovered almost weekly. But researchers generally agree on the basic major Pre-Columbian cultural influences in Arizona and those are shown in the table at right.

Note on discovering new sites: If you happen to come across what you think may be a new archaeology site, please do not disturb anything. Take photos, note the exact location on your map or GPS and notify the office of the State Archaeologist. Your reward is knowing you did the right thing. Also, consider this added bonus: by virtue of doing nothing at such a site you avoid jail time and bad publicity. Archaeology sites—including rock art—are very strictly protected by law.

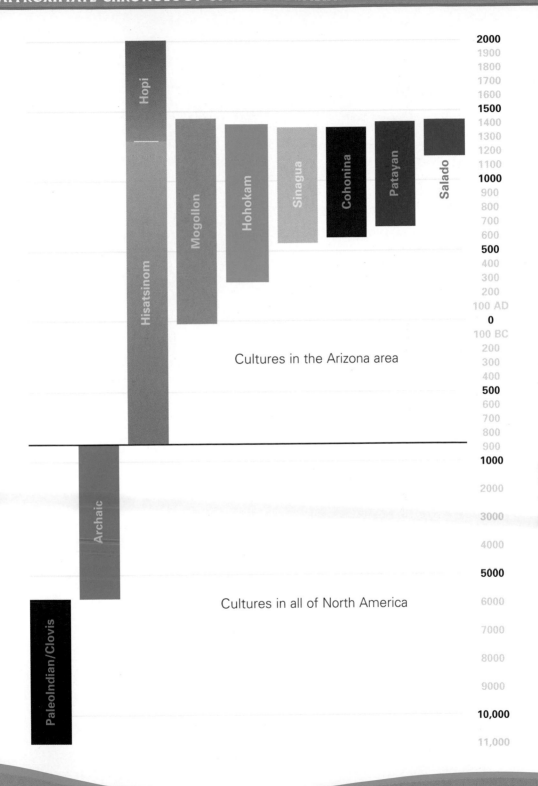

Cultures in the Arizona area

Cultures in all of North America

Paleontology

Paleontology sites on public land are also protected by laws, although the exact details and applications thereof are still being refined by the authorities, most of whom don't know a fossil from a turnip. It is unclear, for example, if you are allowed to collect common invertebrate fossils on certain public lands or not. Regardless, ambiguity in the law does not grant you license to dig fossils on public land. To avoid becoming a casualty in the Great Fossil and Bone Wars of the 21st Century, leave the rocks and fossils where you find them. Remember Big Brother is watching, especially in such places as the Petrified Forest where, at times, there are more "Fossil Cops" than tourists.

Private land is another matter altogether. The law is clear here: Fossils on private land belong to the land owner. You may dig to your paleontological heart's content on private land so long as you have a contract and/or permission from the owner. If you happen to own land where fossils outcrop, you can even commercialize your find by charging other enthusiasts a fee to dig them. So get out there and look for a T-rex on your land; it could be worth a truckload of pesos!

Geology

Arizona has a long geologic history and an important fossil record. The oldest rock in the state is, not surprisingly, at the bottom of the Grand Canyon, while the youngest are Pleistocene and Holocene sediments scattered as thin crusts atop older rocks in river valleys and creek beds.

Arizona is further blessed with a great diversity of geologic provinces, landforms and outcrops. Nearly everywhere you look in this state there are unique and exciting geologic features. Because a large portion of the state is public land, you're welcome to explore many of the wonders of this geologic cornucopia. But let's face it, even in a dozen volumes, there wouldn't be enough room to describe all the great geology here. So we're going to take the easy way out and only discuss the highlights, which are fairly accessible to you. Keep in mind all the archaeology and paleontology sites have some sort of geologic aspect to them, so even if you don't see mention of them in the listing, you'll doubtless enjoy the added geo-bonus free of charge.

	Years (millions)
CENOZOIC ERA	
Holocene Epoch Pleistocene Epoch	
	2
Pliocene Epoch	
	5
Miocene Epoch	
	24
Oligocene Epoch	
	35
Eocene Epoch	
	55
Paleocene Epoch	
MESOZOIC ERA	**65**
Cretaceous Period	
	140
Jurassic Period	
	200
Triassic Period	
PALEOZOIC ERA	**240**
Permian Period	
	290
Carboniferous Period	
	360
Devonian Period	
	410
Silurian Period	
	440
Ordovician Period	
	500
Cambrian Period	
PRECAMBRIAN	**570**
Proterozoic Eon	
	2500
Archean Eon	
	3600
Pre-Archean Eon	
	4500

VISITOR ETIQUETTE

Irreplaceable Treasures

We're quite sure you don't need to be told that the sites you'll visit are fragile, irreplaceable, natural treasures. We're also certain you don't want to hear again and again that these sites need your care in preserving them. And, really, why would we want to use valuable print space to tell you how important it is for you to take an interest in conserving these sites for future generations when we all know you understand and practice that already? What with all those laws and societal taboos in place to ward off destructive behavior, who in their right mind would even consider such negligence? Certainly not you or us. But you never know. You may come across someone who doesn't understand these things—say a social deviant, cultural moron, or an alleged human with the collective intelligence of a brick. If you do, you can just show them this paragraph and try to set them on the straight and narrow path. God smiles on those who help preserve the Earth.

Do Not Disturb

Let's suppose you stumble across a huge pile of broken pottery or a petrified log weathered into thousands of fragments at a place not mentioned in this or any other guidebook. You might reason that pocketing just one tiny piece or two couldn't possibly impact the site as a whole, considering the uncountable abundance still left undisturbed, right? No, not right. In fact, VERY not right. If every visitor took just one tiny piece then soon there would be nothing left except an empty hole where once there was a dinosaur skeleton or a cliff dwelling. So please don't disturb any sites. Future generations will thank you. And you'll be doing your part in relieving overcrowded prisons by not becoming an inmate.

On the Rez

All Indian reservations have their own rules and regulations, which are up to you to be aware of and follow. The Navajo Indian reservation in particular is a sovereign nation with their own laws and law enforcement officials. As with any nation, it's up to you to know and abide by the rules. If you plan to spend any amount of time on a reservation, we strongly advise you to read up on the tribal culture first. Becoming familiar with tribal customs and etiquette will serve you well. On the "Rez" things run a bit differently than in the outside world and that's a good thing. Keep in mind that arrogance, stubbornness and haste have no place on the Rez. Remember the following while in these areas:

- Never supply alcohol or drugs to anyone, including those on the Rez. Many reservations are "dry" and it's against the law to even possess liquor (yes, even beer).

- Do not give money to panhandlers here or in any tourist area.

- Never offer a ride to a hitchhiker here or anywhere else. Some people are very bold and will come right up to your car to try and coerce you into giving them a lift. Although it can be tempting to give money or a ride to someone who appears in need, it's best to avoid this. Be respectful and firm in your denial.

- Avoid driving at night. Many of the roads are in poor condition and there is no lighting. Most of the land is open range (that means no fences—allowing animals to roam at will) and you really, really, really do not want to hit a cow with your car. And remember, there are more drunk drivers on the road after dark.

- While some social ceremonies on the reservation are open to visitors, it is important to show respect by not discussing the ceremonies and by dressing appropriately.

- Two differences observed between native and non-native cultures involve eye contact and touch. Eye contact among some Native American cultures is considered impolite and touching outside of family or friends a sign of disrespect. Even a firm grip in a handshake may be seen as over-bearing and a light touch is preferred.

- Most Native American cultures consider it offensive to have their photos taken. Do not take any photos or video while on the Rez without first obtaining permission.

PRECAUTIONS

Hot or Cold Bring Lots of Water

Arizona is both hot AND cold, depending on where you go and when. And it can be either one in a big way. It's no secret that Arizona can get downright sizzling during the daytime, especially from May–September with the oft-heard "But it's a dry heat!" little consolation when the mercury zooms past 110 degrees. Bring plenty of drinking water, even in winter. Many of these sites are remote and have no water supply. Here's a lesson in common desert-traveler sense: just because a site is named something provocative like "Laws Spring" doesn't mean there's

a spring there. Or, if there is, it may be undrinkable (such IS the case with Laws Spring: the water there is a fetid slime pool). Also, we've jumped on to the Better Health Bandwagon and are promoting a reduction in skin cancer, so stock up on sunscreen and wear a wide-brim hat.

If you're camping in the desert, be aware that it can get chilly at night, even in the summer. In the winter, the higher elevations and northern plateaus can become veritable "Ice Station Zebra" with temps down into the teens not uncommon. And don't forget the wind! With much of the state lacking in tree cover, the wind can become a major force to be reckoned with, especially if it's cold. As they say in Minnesota, "Bring warm clothes!"

Flash Floods

Do not enter any canyon, creek, river, or wash if there is a chance of rain in the region. Read that last sentence again and pick up on the word "region," meaning not just the immediate area, but anyplace within the watershed of your area. This is especially important in "slots" such as Antelope Canyon where 11 people died in a single flash flood a few years ago from a thunderstorm a half dozen miles away. Some of the bodies were never found.

Rock Fall

Remember that story in 2003 about Aron Ralston, the explorer who was climbing through a canyon when a loose boulder shifted and pinned him against the wall? He was trapped for days before he finally did the unthinkable and cut off his own arm with a pocket knife so he could escape. He made it out alive, but just barely. In the wilds, the dynamics of weathering ensure a continual supply of loose rock and precariously balanced boulders. We recommend you do not tempt fate by scrambling around off established routes. If you do take the path less traveled be sure to hike with a companion. We want you to come home with all your limbs and with stories a little less harrowing than Aron's.

Sandstorms

The desert is a dusty, sandy place and we all know that. Although bad sandstorms are infrequent, keep in mind anytime the wind really kicks up it can be hell-to-pay for car paint finishes, eyeglass coatings and the desire to maintain a modicum of personal hygiene. During a really good

"blow," sand and dust are entrained into the air dozens of feet off the surface. It can get so thick it blocks out the sun, all the while penetrating your vehicle like an insidious vapor. When its over, you'll find ultra-fine sand grains in every nook and cranny as well as all unsealed, air-tight containers. Don't try eating a sandwich while driving through a sandstorm! You'll be inadvertently grinding your enamel away after the first few bites. There's not much you can do if caught in one. Just grin—with mouth tightly closed—and bear it.

Roads

A great many of the sites we list are accessible by pavement and/or maintained gravel roads. Many others are attained via unimproved dirt tracts that can be dicey in bad weather, even for 4WD. We strongly recommend you check locally about road conditions before heading out to remote sites. If you don't, you may be in for a long hike back out and enormous tow-truck charges. Most of these sites do not need special vehicles (such as the Swiss Army truck pictured here) but be sure to use caution anywhere the road is unmaintained.

Animals

Most of the time you'll not encounter bothersome animals. However, in the summer months, certain threatening critters come out to play.

Scorpions, tarantulas, rattlesnakes, Gila Monsters and bees are potentially harmful to humans. Remember, you are just a visitor in their world, so tread softly. With a little common sense we can all get along. Keep an eye out—don't put your hands or feet where you cannot see them, especially under rocks or in crevasses.

LEFT MIDDLE: Tarantulas are a common sight, especially in summer.

LEFT BOTTOM: Many species of colorful lizards are watching you!

Plants

Plants of the desert are another matter altogether. Cactus are ubiquitous throughout the state. Be careful where you tread. DO NOT sit on the ground without first checking the spot or you may find yourself asking a travel partner to pick spines out of your sorry butt (believe me, I've been there and it ain't pretty!). Teddy Bear Cholla are especially diabolic with clusters of spring-loaded spines just waiting for you to brush against them. If

Teddy bear cholla. Do not hug these!

you do, you'll never forget it as dozens of barbed needles launch right through your clothes deep into your skin. And that's only the beginning of the fun. Removing them is another matter. Just keep your distance from cactus and you'll be fine.

Saguaro cactus in bloom.

Barrel cactus (above) and prickly pears welcome you to the desert.

Valley Fever

If you don't live in the Southwest you probably have never heard of coccidioidomycosis, aka "valley fever," a strange and sometimes lethal fungal infection endemic to the deserts of Arizona and California. "cocci," as it's called in the medical trade, occurs after breathing in spores of a particular fungus (*Coccidioides immitis*), which lay dormant in the dirt. Generally, you have to inhale a large amount of these spores for valley fever to manifest itself in a meaningful way. That's why most of the public health problems are restricted to people who spend a lot of time digging, i.e., construction workers, archaeologists, geology students and the like. If you don't expose yourself to a lot of airborne dust, chances are you need not be concerned. But if, after visiting the desert, you come down with flu-like symptoms and it isn't flu season, get checked immediately. Take it from me—I nearly died at age 26 from it— cocci is no laughing matter.

Saguaro cactus

THE BEST OF ARIZONA

If you had to choose just one site from each category that was the absolute top of its class, which would it be? The following are our choices for the best of the best of ancient Arizona.

Archaeology—Canyon De Chelly

There are many very excellent archaeological sites in Arizona. The problem is picking one place that best represents the diversity and quality of the archaeological experience. The runner-up spot in the competition has to be a tie between Monument Valley and Navajo National Monument. But the winner, for our money anyway, is Canyon De Chelly, the place that has it all: cliff dwellings, petroglyphs, pictographs, caves, ruins of all kinds and everything in an idyllic canyon setting that is yet inhabited by native people. Best of all, it's not Disney-fied, the experience is unforgettable and access is no hassle.

Paleontology—Petrified Forest

Despite its plenitude of rock exposures, Arizona is not so famous for its fossil record. Yes, there are many superb prehistoric specimens that have been unearthed here but most sites are remote or not open to the public. Yet what it lacks in quantity, Arizona makes up for in quality with the Petrified Forest. Maybe you've seen "petrified forests" in other places (seems like nearly every state has one), but if you haven't been here you haven't seen The Petrified Forest, far and away the most impressive one on the planet. The beauty of the fossils and the setting they are in are unsurpassed. And it has some great archaeology sites to boot.

 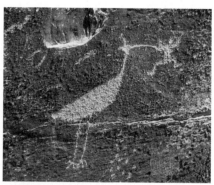

Geology—Grand Canyon

If you cannot, of your own accord, name the singular outstanding geologic site of Arizona then you need to retake third-grade geography class. The Grand Canyon is perhaps the most amazing geologic site you'll ever see. It attracts millions of visitors from around the world every year and if you're not one of them, then there's only one person to blame. Don't even think of leaving this planet before seeing it.

Panoramic view of the Grand Canyon from Pima Point on the West Rim Drive. Grand Canyon National Park NPS photo

View the remains of an ancestral Puebloan Village at Tusayan Museum, 23 miles east of Grand Canyon Village. Grand Canyon National Park NPS photo

AGUA FRIA NATIONAL MONUMENT

Directions:
From Phoenix, follow I-17 north about 45 miles to exit #256 (the Badger Springs interchange) then east into the monument. There is no visitor center or improved trails at this time.

Contact Info:
BLM Phoenix Field Office
602-417-9200
www.blm.gov/az/st/en/prog/blm_special_areas/natmon/afria.html

Fee: no fees because there's nothing in the way of infrastructure

Hours: daily

Best time to visit:
not advisable if rain is predicted; avoid midsummer heat

Camping/Lodging:
primitive camping only; closest lodging is Prescott or Camp Verde

Access: moderate to extreme; most roads need 4WD

Jon's Rating: ★★★✦✩ (archaeology)
★★★✦✩ (geology)

Jon's Notes:
This as-yet-undeveloped gem of the archeological world is now a 71,000-acre national monument, with some of the most significant prehistoric sites in the state. Over 400 different sites and 4 major settlements have been documented within its boundaries. The area is very rugged and relatively isolated. Presently, there are no facilities or improved trails and, consequently, no fees or permits are required for hiking or camping. Vehicles must stay on designated roadways. Do not attempt to travel this area without a high-clearance vehicle and lots of water—fresh water sources are rare.

Even the namesake river—Agua Fria—is short on agua most of the year. If you wish to visit some of the archeological sites in Agua Fria, contact one of the jeep tour companies in Flagstaff or Sedona. Stay tuned for upcoming developments, the National Park Service has big plans for this place.

LEFT: Although most of the monument is yet inaccessible, petroglyphs are found in many places. These are at Badger Springs.

ABOVE: Pueblo La Plata is way out in the no mans land of the eastern monument. The trek there will teach your vehicle a thing or two about off-road driving.

RIGHT: Pottery shards litter many sites.

Badger Springs Petroglyphs

One excellent Agua Fria locale worth visiting and relatively easy to access is Badger Springs rock art site. The beginning is a dirt road accessible with a regular car in dry weather only. From I-17, take the Badger Springs exit into the Monument. Park at the trailhead, about 2 miles from the interstate. Follow the apparent creek bed downstream on foot (an easy and pleasant hike in dry weather) for about one mile until it joins with Agua Fria River. At this junction, look to your left for petroglyphs of animals and abstract figures located about 30 feet above the stream bed.

Badger Springs petroglyphs are a short scenic hike from the parking area.

ANTELOPE CANYON

Directions:
Antelope Canyon is about 3 miles east of Page on Rt. 98. Since this is Navajo tribal land, you must have a native Navajo guide, whom you can hire in the area of the canyon or in Page.

Contact Info:
Navajo Nation Parks
928-871-6647
www.navajonationparks.org

Fee: you must hire a Navajo guide and/or have a permit

Hours: daylight hours

Best time to visit:
anytime EXCEPT when rain is predicted in the area—do not ignore this vital warning!

Camping/Lodging:
none available on the Navajo Reservation but both nearby in Page

Access: easy to extreme depending on how wild you want to get

Jon's Rating: ★★★★★ (geology)

Jon's Notes: This is perhaps the most visited and extensively photographed slot canyon in the world, and for good reason. When sunlight penetrates its depths, Antelope Canyon becomes a veritable kaleidoscope of nature with rainbow colors and subtly textured layers. The canyon has two sections divided by Rt. 98. The Upper Canyon, south of 98, is accessed by a sandy wash (look for the trinket stands marking the entrance!). You used to be able to hike in on your own but on our last visit only authorized jeeps were allowed, although this may change. The more impressive Lower Canyon runs north of 98 into Lake Powell and, if you are so inclined, can be a hike/climb of several miles. It is a much more strenuous workout and requires climbing in and out via ropes or ladders bolted to the canyon wall. In either case, you need a guide since you are on Navajo land. If you enjoy the experience, ask the locals about other slot canyons nearby; there are several. Remember—all slot canyons can be dangerous. If rain is predicted anywhere in the region, DO NOT ENTER! Flash floods (from a thunderstorm 5 miles away) killed 11 people here in August of 1997.

LEFT: It's no wonder why Antelope Canyon is one of the most famous natural sites in the world.

*Visit during midday
and the sun beams
enliven the light show
even more.*

Just Add No Water

When you mention sand most people in North America think of sandy river channels and ocean beaches. But this place was neither—having formed originally as extensive sand dune environments not unlike the Sahara Desert. The multicolored rock layers that accumulated in this area are part of the Glen Canyon Group, which consist of cross-bedded sandstones formed during the Jurassic Period about 200 million years ago. Thousands of feet of sand piled up, eventually compressing into the rock evident here. The bright hues are a result of iron oxides coloring the sedimentary layers.

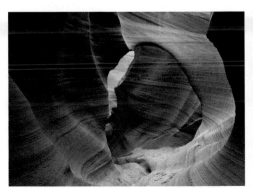

It's tempting to ignore the weather when something this spectacular is along your travel route. But if rain is predicted, don't even think of entering a slot canyon such as this—the consequences could be fatal.

ANTELOPE HILL PETROGLYPHS

3

Directions:
From Yuma, follow I-8 east about 38 miles to exit #37 at Avenue 36E. Head north toward Roll and obvious hill with large white "A" on its side. At 2 miles you'll see a working quarry on the west side of the hill. Turn right after the quarry to gravel lot on north side with signage.

Contact Info:
Bureau of Reclamation
928-317-3200
www.visityuma.com/rocks_petroglyphs.html

Fee: free

Hours: daily

Best time to visit:
not advisable if rain is predicted; avoid midsummer heat

Camping/Lodging: basic camping on BLM land

Access: good road; easy to moderate hiking

Jon's Rating: ★★☆☆☆ (archaeology)

Jon's Notes:
This site features dozens of petroglyphs etched into rhyolite boulders outcropping along the edge of an ancient lava flow beside the Gila River. Several grinding stones—metates—are also nearby. Researchers speculate the older petroglyphs may have been carved more than 2,000 years ago, but the major use of this site was from about AD 500 to the mid-1800s when white settlers drove out the Indians in the name of progress. And the progress continues with quarry operations! Judging by the layout of the site and their proximity to the giant hole in the hillside, the need for road gravel no-doubt led to the pulverizing of many fine petroglyphs.

LEFT: Basalt makes for a good canvas at Antelope Hill.

BESH-BA-GOWAH ARCHAEOLOGICAL PARK ④

Directions:
Located just south of downtown Globe. Take Broad Street south from Hwy. 60 and follow the signs.

Contact Info:
City of Globe
Visitor information
928-425-0320 or 800-804-5623
www.jqjacobs.net/southwest/besh_ba_gowah.html

Fee: per person or group entrance fee

Hours: daily

Best time to visit: anytime

Camping/Lodging: both nearby in Globe

Access: easy

Jon's Rating: ★★★★★ (archaeology)

Jon's Notes:
In 1948, the Army Corps of Engineers displayed uncanny ability for governmental lunacy by bulldozing a large portion of Besh-Ba-Gowah ruins to smooth the ground for a group of Boy Scouts wishing to erect tents. Despite this stupendous example of bureaucratic buffoonery, Besh-Ba-Gowah has become one of the finest archeological sites in Arizona—tracing a history of occupation from as early as AD 750. The park consists of an excellent visitor center/museum that houses a major collection of artifacts from the site. Parts of the adjacent 700-year-old pueblo have been accurately reconstructed and come complete with furnishings typical of the period (sorry, no time-share rentals are available at this time). Besh-Ba-Gowah is thought to have been a major cultural and ceremonial center for the Salado culture, which thrived here from about AD 1200–1400. There's even a botanical garden that features native plants used by the Salado people.

LEFT: In spite of Corps of Engineers stupidity, some parts of Besh-Ba-Gowah have been saved.

Some of the park's structures have been faithfully reconstructed to the way they were 800–900 years ago.

Boom Town

Besh-Ba-Gowah likely originated as something of a prehistoric "boom town" along the ancient trade route between Casas Grandes, Mexico and the Salt River region of Arizona, which thrived from AD 1100–1450. The decision to construct a pueblo here was at least partly based on the abundant clean water supplied by a nearby permanent spring (now extinct), in addition to the river itself. At the time there was more annual rainfall and sufficient arable land to meet the needs of the large population. A severe drought from AD 1276–1299 caused a decline in the population and by AD 1400 the pueblo was abandoned.

One of the best archaeological parks in the state is right in Globe.

CANYON DE CHELLY

5

Directions:
Located 3 miles east of Chinle on Arizona Rt. 7. If you miss it you have an attention problem or a seriously impaired GPS in your car.

Contact Info:
National Park Service
Visitor information
928-674-5500
www.nps.gov/cach

Fee:
free access to the rim drives and overlooks; to enter the canyon you must hire a Navajo guide and a 4WD vehicle (if you aren't driving one)

Hours:
hours vary but they are generally 8am–5pm, closed on Christmas Day

Best time to visit: anytime

Camping/Lodging:
both near the entrance; basic camping at Cottonwood Campground is free and by donation

Access:
easy to very difficult; take an easy 4WD vehicle tour or hike for more of a workout; on the South Rim, you may hike down into the canyon and visit Whitehouse Ruin for free; there are also horseback trips

Jon's Rating: ★★★★☆ (geology)
★★★★★ (archaeology)

Jon's Notes:
With its breathtaking cliff dwellings, multitude of incredible ruins, scores of fine rock art panels and postcard-perfect settings, Canyon de Chelly (pronounced Canyon d' Shay) is undoubtedly the preeminent archeological site of Arizona and one of the finest anywhere. It is, in fact, not a single site but a collection of some 2,500 scattered along a group of canyons collectively known as Canyon De Chelly. The Canyon has been more-or-less continuously inhabited for over 2,000 years. Although managed by the National Park Service, the Canyon is owned by the Navajo Nation and many of them still live and work within its walls. If you're looking for impressive ruins in a picture-book setting, this is the place. You could spend a full week here and not see it all. Whatever time you spend will be unforgettable.

LEFT: Whitehouse Ruin is one of the most well known of Canyon De Chelly's many excellent archaeology sites.

ABOVE: On the trail to
Whitehouse Ruin.

RIGHT: At the bottom,
you're deposited right
in front of the ruin..

The Long Walk

Archaic Indians began frequenting this area nearly 5,000 years ago, living in seasonal shelters along the canyon walls. About 2,500 years later, members of the Basketmaker culture began practicing agriculture here. This led to a reliable source of plant foods and induced a more stationary existence. Basketmaker farmers lived happily in dispersed hamlets throughout the canyons. Around AD 750, for reasons unclear, the concept of a centralized village became popular. Possibly as a defensive measure, ancestral Pueblo peoples built the well-known cliff dwellings and occupied them until about AD 1300 when most of the populace abruptly decamped. The Navajo, migrating from the north, entered the area about AD 1700 and lived within the idyllic canyons until 1864 when Colonel Kit Carson mounted a brutal military campaign against them. The U.S. forces slaughtered many of the Canyon de Chelly Navajo and burned their homes, crops and legendary peach orchards. Those who were captured were forced to walk over 300 miles to Fort Sumner in New Mexico—an ordeal called "The Long Walk" by those who endured it.

The Canyon De Chelly inhabitants were advanced ceramic artists. (Artwork by Vernon Morris)

ABOVE: The hike to
Whitehouse Ruin
begins at the overlook
parking lot on the
South Rim Drive.

RIGHT: The Navajo
spent a great deal of
effort carving trails and
tunnels through the
sandstone on the way
to the canyon floor so
folks like you can view
Whitehouse Ruin.
You'd be remiss not to
show your appreciation
by hiking this trek with
incredible views and
buying some jewelry
from the artists at
the bottom.

Don't Be A Scrooge

There's not many opportunities to get something for nothing in this world but the Navajo have done a lot to provide you with just that. First, you could camp here free, although we strongly encourage you to make a donation in the box to support the local economy. In addition, if you are such a sissy tight-wad and cultural Scrooge determined to not spend a dime, you can visit Canyon De Chelly's most famous ruin absolutely free of charge. The 3-mile round trip follows a moderately difficult scenic trail from Whitehouse Overlook. It descends 700 feet through tunnels and picturesque switch-backs to the canyon floor and deposits you right at the base of the ruins. But as you enjoy this splendor, keep in mind the Navajo spent a helluva lot of energy literally carving this trail into the canyon wall by hand. If you can't find it in your heart to give up a few greenbacks for the cause, then you're not the person we thought you were when you got this book. In fact, you probably stole it! Shame on you...

The 3-mile round-trip hike to Whitehouse Ruin is one of the more scenic hikes in Arizona.

Your reward at the bottom. But you now have to hike back UP to your car!

CASA GRANDE RUINS

6

Directions:
One would think Casa Grande Ruins would be in Casa Grande, but it's not. It's in Coolidge, some 17 miles to the northeast. In fact, it's not even in Coolidge proper, but lies about a mile north of the city off Arizona Rt. 87.

Contact Info:
National Park Service
Visitor information
520-723-3172
www.nps.gov/cagr

Fee: per person or group entrance fee

Hours: daily 8am–5pm

Best time to visit: anytime; avoid midsummer heat

Camping/Lodging: not in monument, but both are nearby

Access: easy

Jon's Rating: ★★★★★ (archaeology)

Jon's Notes:
Built by Hohokam Indians sometime between AD 1150–1350, this intriguing location encompasses 60 prehistoric sites including the ultra famous 4-story Great House for which the site is named (actually it's only 3 stories—the first story is a platform about five feet high, which serves to raise the whole structure above its surroundings). The precise function of the intriguing Great House is not known but it's possible this marvel of ancient architecture served as an astronomical observatory. It is a perfect 3:4 rectangle oriented along the cardinal points of the compass. At certain times, such as the winter solstice, one of its precisely crafted windows aligns with the setting sun. Other alignments may coincide with agricultural cycles. Some researchers also speculate the Great House was home to the high priests of the community. If so, they lived like Bill Gates and had a helluva view from their penthouse.

LEFT: At about 800 years old and completely exposed to the weather for most of its existence, Casa Grande is remarkably intact.

Not only are there excellent ruins, but there's some great pottery as well.

(Artwork by Vernon Morris)

Villains in the House

In the 1800s and early 1900s, before anyone ever took this site seriously, looters and pot hunters wreaked havoc with Casa Grande by digging holes willy-nilly and destroying many parts of the structure in search of the Holy Grail. Some of these same bozos were also idiot enough to carve their names into the main structure's fragile walls. But, thanks to these buffoons, we have the opportunity, one hundred years later, to see how such handiwork accelerates degradation of archeological sites. Thankfully, the site has now gained some respect and is being well cared for by the National Park Service.

The park service has built a roof over the structure to help protect it from the elements.

CASA MALPAIS

7

Directions:
The ruins are located just north of Springerville off U.S. 60. You must check in at the visitor center and museum on Main Street first and be guided at the site.

Contact Info:
City of Springerville
Visitor information
928-333-5375
www.wmonline.com/attract/casam.htm

Fee: per person or group tour fee

Hours: variable—call ahead

Best time to visit: anytime; avoid midsummer heat

Camping/Lodging: camping and lodging nearby in Springerville

Access:
mostly easy to moderate 1-mile round-trip hike around ruins; the optional climb through the lava flow is more difficult but fun

Jon's Rating: ★★★★✦ (archaeology)

Jon's Notes:
The Spanish term malpais roughly translates to "badland" and often is used in reference to deserts and other forbidding environments. In this case, the landscape is the remains of an old lava flow and the term malpais is not much in order, considering its location adjacent to the Little Colorado River and fertile flood plains thereof. This 16-acre site was built upon by the Mogollon culture who occupied it from roughly AD 1250–1350. It consists of a large stone pueblo, a Great Kiva, numerous isolated rooms, ceremonial chambers, rock art panels, grinding stones and a unique basalt stairway set into a crevasse in the ancient lava bed. The visitor center/museum, located on Main Street in downtown Springerville, controls all access to the site.

LEFT: A trip to the upper reaches of the site follows an ancient stairway through the lava flow.

ABOVE: The site is atop a lava terrace overlooking the valley of the Little Colorado.

RIGHT: Petroglyphs also abide among the basalt boulders here.

Living Over Catacombs

One of the more unique aspects of Casa Malpais are the catacombs situated under the living structures themselves. These are the result of giant cracks forming in the lava flow long before the Indians came around. The catacombs are interconnected fissures that apparently had a variety of important functions for the natives, not the least of which was the venting of smoke from fires in the living areas above. An estimated 200 burials were tucked away into the crevasses. Though you might be concerned with having your house sitting atop an open-pit burial vault—with its pungent decay odors and associated vermin—you'll be happy to know the stench was somewhat mitigated by smoke coursing through the chambers. Hooray for modern HVAC!

Excellent ceramics have been found among the ruins of this site. (Artwork by Vernon Morris)

CHIRICAHUA NATIONAL MONUMENT

8

Directions:
From Willcox take Arizona 186 south for 31 miles to junction with Arizona 181. Be alert and beware—this is mostly open-range country where you are likely to encounter animals on the road. (Believe me, you DO NOT want to hit a cow with your car!) Turn north 4 miles to entrance gate.

Contact Info:
National Park Service
Visitor information
520-824-3560
www.nps.gov/chir

Fee: per person entrance fee

Hours: Visitor Center open daily 8am–4:30pm

Best time to visit: anytime; avoid midsummer heat

Camping/Lodging:
basic camping in monument; closest lodging is in Willcox

Access:
the roads from Willcox cross many fords which are subject to flash flooding—do not attempt this drive if significant rain is predicted in the area; once in the monument, the trails range from easy to very difficult

Jon's Rating: ★★★★⯪ (geology)

Jon's Notes:
Twenty seven million years ago, the gods got a little miffed about something and, in a fit of volcanic anger, shook the land around Chiricahua National Monument with an immense eruption that eventually laid down two thousand feet of ash and pumice. This mixture fused into a rock called *rhyolitic tuff* and eventually eroded into the weird pinnacles, strange spires, precariously balanced boulders, twisted arches and a host of other unusual rock formations seen here today. Chiricahua features 17 miles of maintained trails in a monument that is 87% wilderness.

LEFT: Does this place scream sci-fi or what?!

The rocks have had their coffee and are patiently awaiting your inspection.

Standup Guys

The Apaches call Chiricahua "The Land of Standing-Up Rocks," which is a fitting description for this incredible lithologic sci-fi landscape. The wild formations you see here are not rare in the geologic world—it's just that they don't happen in such profusion in many other places. The primary progenitor of this anomalous landscape is *differential weathering*, a geologic process whereby weaker rock is selectively removed from the whole, leaving the stronger sections exposed. Differential weathering is the culprit for many of Arizona's wonderful landforms including Monument Valley. The Grand Canyon is its most spectacular achievement.

Other places may have some similar geology but not nearly in this abundance or diversity in one place.

CLOVER RUIN

9

Directions:
From downtown Williams, head west on Railroad Ave. about one mile. At the top of the hill turn left before I-40 toward Williams District Ranger Station. Follow the signs and frontage road down the hill about ½ mile. Turn left toward the Ranger Station and make your first right. Park at the old CCC office building. The site is just to the right of this building behind the information kiosk that has no information.

Contact Info:
Kaibab National Forest
800-863-0546
www.fs.fcd.us/r3/kai/oldrec/sites_wc_clover.html

Fee: no fees because there ain't much here

Hours: daylight hours

Best time to visit: anytime

Camping/Lodging:
basic camping in Kaibab Forest; developed camping and lodging nearby in Williams

Access: as easy as it gets

Jon's Rating: ★✫☆☆☆ (archaeology)

Jon's Notes:
One could question if Clover Ruin even qualifies as an archaeological "site" at all, but someone obviously found it interesting enough to excavate and reconstruct. The dwelling, such as it is, is presumed to

have been built by Cohonina culture people who occupied it for a brief time some 1,000 years ago before racing off into the wild blue yonder. This is one of those sites that leave you asking more questions like "Are we there yet?" or "When do we eat?" The city of Williams is finally on the archaeological tour map!

LEFT and ABOVE: It may not look like much, but at least it's within city limits!

Directions:
From Douglas, take U.S. 80 two miles to U.S. 191. Go north approximately 45 miles to Sun Sites, then turn left (west) on Ironwood Road. Continue on Ironwood Road (which becomes Forest Road 84 at the Forest boundary) for 8 miles to Cochise Stronghold Campground.

Contact Info:
Coronado National Forest/Douglas Ranger District
Visitor information
520-364-3468
www.fs.fed.us/r3/coronado

Fee: entrance fee at campground and picnic area

Hours: daily

Best time to visit: anytime

Camping/Lodging:
camping only within the park; closest lodging is in Benson or Willcox

Access:
easy to very difficult; road is good to campground; hike to Council Rocks is long and difficult

Jon's Rating: ★★★☆☆ (geology)
★★⯪☆☆ (archaeology)

Jon's Notes:
Located in the Dragoon Mountains east of Tucson, Cochise Stronghold and, specifically, Council Rocks, is reputed to be the place where legendary Indian warrior Cochise held council meetings with his followers and other tribal leaders—including the great Geronimo—during their struggle for self-preservation in the mid-1800s. Later, at the same site, Cochise met General Howard and agreed to peace with the U.S. government. Cochise is reputed to be the only Indian resistance leader who was not coerced, captured, or killed by government forces during the 19th century. Council Rocks may be accessed by a long (12 miles one-way), difficult hike from the campground. You might also ask at the park for directions and road conditions on the west side of the Dragoons. The hike is much shorter to Council Rocks from the west, IF you can get close with a vehicle.

LEFT: It's a nice place to have a stronghold, don't you think?

In the heart of the Dragoon Mountains, Cochise and his band of warriors held out against the mighty U.S. Calvary until a negotiated settlement finally brought an end to the hostilities.

Painting for Posterity

The original pictographs at Council Rocks are believed to be the work of Mogollon culture people over 1,000 years ago, long before the legendary figure of Cochise appeared. But, like many famous rock art sites in picturesque settings, there were likely several generations of artisans that did their thing here. Some of the images are obviously more recent than others and may even have been executed during Cochise's time.

Two of the greatest legendary figures in Indian history met here to discuss tactics over 100 years ago. LEFT: Cochise; RIGHT: Geronimo (Artwork by Vernon Morris)

COLOSSAL CAVE MOUNTAIN PARK

11

Directions:
From Tucson, take I-10 east to exit #279 (the Vail/Wentworth exit), turn north and follow the signs for about 7 miles to the park entrance.

Contact Info:
Pima County Park
Visitor information
520-647-PARK (7275)
www.colossalcave.com

Fee: per person or group admission fee

Hours: summer: 8am–6pm; winter: 9am–5pm

Best time to visit: anytime

Camping/Lodging:
overnight camping permitted but there are no hook-ups for RVs; lodging in Tucson

Access: easy

Jon's Rating: ★★★✫✫ (geology)
★★★✫✫ (archaeology)

Jon's Notes:
What is it about cowboys who go out looking for lost cattle? It seems like they have all the luck! Colossal Cave is another one of those stories where a rancher—this one named Solomon Lick— discovers a gigantic, mysterious hole in the ground while searching for bovines that strayed from the herd. That was 1879 and since then the cave has attracted the attention of everyone from train robbers to university presidents. The first tours were taken through the unimproved cave in 1923. In the mid-1930s the Civilian Conservation Corps (CCC) constructed most of the buildings, walkways and wiring, which made modern tours possible. One of the great things about this park are the efforts to preserve both the prehistoric and historic aspects.

LEFT: The Grand Dame of underground Arizona.

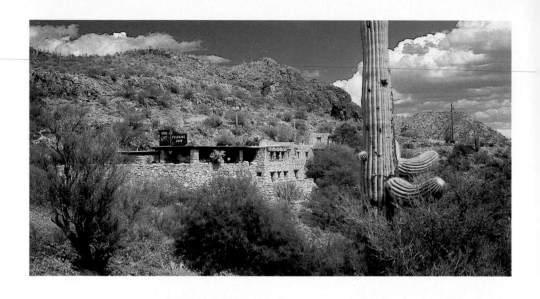

Not far from Tucson—up a hill, down a hole...

Dry Caves

Colossal Cave, like Grand Canyon Caverns, is a "dry" cave, which means the formations here are no longer actively forming. Despite this fact, or maybe because of it, there are great examples of stalactites, stalagmites and most of the other requisite speleothems worthy of viewing. While most caves hold at temps in the mid-50s, the thermometer here stays a nice 70 degrees year-round. The park serves as an active research facility for archaeologists—the cave was used by local tribes intermittently from about AD 800 to the early 1800s. It also hosts research projects for biologists and naturalists (there are some species of rare bats that live in the caves) as well as geologists.

The cavern offered ideal shelter to native cultures in the area for many years.

DEER VALLEY PETROGLYPH PRESERVE

12

Directions:
Located in Phoenix. From I-17 take exit #215B; go west on Deer Valley Rd. Just after intersection with 35th Ave, take right fork to parking area.

Contact Info:
Deer Valley Petroglyph Preserve
623-582-8007
https://shesc.asu.edu/dvpp

Fee: per person or group admission fee

Hours: variable—call ahead

Best time to visit: anytime; avoid midsummer heat

Camping/Lodging: developed camping and lodging in Phoenix

Access: easy

Jon's Rating: ★★★★☆ (archaeology)

Jon's Notes:
The most amazing thing about Deer Valley Petroglyph Preserve is the fact it's not a Wal-Mart Supercenter. The result of a joint effort between the Army Corps of Engineers, the Flood Control District of Maricopa County, and Arizona State University, the site preserves 47 acres of boulders and rock in the midst of thriving metro sprawl is, well, astounding. But they did just that and you're the better for it once you visit this major force in the rock art world. The center of attention, of course, is about 1,500 petroglyphs carved between 5000 BC and AD 1400. There are loads of educational programs and a great visitor center/museum. Bring your binoculars for the best viewing.

A variety of images are found at this site. The most famous is the so-called "kissing deer", shown in the right photo.

LEFT: It's not Wal-Mart, and that's a good thing.

It may not be like the games found in the toy section of K-Mart, but the educational programs here can be just as fun and they're a whole lot better for you and your kids.

Get With the Program

In something of a departure from "business as usual" state politics, this site is administered by Arizona State University in cooperation with the Flood Control District. The educational programs are meant to inform you not only of the history of rock art here, but also the major crosscultural message. Emphasis is placed on appreciating cultural artistic expression no matter what form it may take or who may have fashioned it. On select days, knowledgeable docents are on site to help visitors learn about the site, the petroglyphs, and the people who crafted them.

"The Kissing Deer" petroglyph made this place famous.

EAGAR PETROGLYPHS

13

Directions:
From Springerville, follow U.S. 180 south to Eagar (right next door). Turn west on Arizona 260 and follow for 5½ miles. Turn left onto gravel road toward South Fork Campground and X Diamond Ranch. In 1½ miles look for petroglyphs on a face just along north side of road. More occur intermittently from this point west along the basalt boulders and columns.

Contact Info:
call X Diamond Ranch for more info: phone 928-333-2286
www.XDiamondRanch.com

Fee: free

Hours: daylight hours

Best time to visit: anytime except when raining or snowing

Camping/Lodging:
camping at nearby South Fork Campground; exceptional lodging at X Diamond Ranch.

Access: easy to moderate

Jon's Rating: ★★★☆☆ (archaeology)

Jon's Notes:
You may not care, but the lava caprock that outcrops here is called the Springerville Basalt and it runs for miles along the Little Colorado River west of Eagar/Springerville. Those that did care were prehistoric artists who lived in the region a millennia ago. As far as they were concerned the basalt made for a continual blank canvas. Being the creative sort they were, the ancients which frequented this area some 800–1000 years ago, took to the rock with gusto and scribed countless images on the ancient lava bed from Springerville to Greer and beyond. Thomas Kinkade himself would be proud of what these ancient prolific artists did if only he would venture out of his fantasy world for a few moments and see it.

LEFT: Batman or Robin? You tell me.

The images are found on cliffs and boulders overlooking the Little Colorado.

Larger Than Rhode Island!

If you look at a black-and-white map of the Springerville Volcanic Field, you'd think someone's ink pen burst and splattered all over the paper. Over 400 cones and vents dot the landscape in an area of roughly 1,200 square miles. As the brochure says "That's larger than the state of Rhode Island!"—which is a pretty meaningless comparison since most of us have never been to Rhode Island. Although the last eruption here was 700,000 years ago, it gives you a glimpse of one of North America's great dormant volcanic hot spots. Be sure to visit the Little Bear Archaeological Site right nearby on the X Diamond Ranch.

Petroglyphs of animals and all sorts of "other things" are found here.

ELDEN PUEBLO

14

Directions:
Elden Pueblo is located one mile north of the Flagstaff Mall on the west side of U.S. Highway 89 North, just south of its junction with Townsend-Winona Road. A sign for "Elden Pueblo Ruins" leads into the parking lot. Follow the obvious trail from the parking area, south to the ruins.

Contact Info:
Coconino National Forest
Visitor information
928-527-3452
www.fs.fed.us/r3/coconino/recreation/peaks/elden-pueblo.shtml

Fee:
there are fees to participate in the supervised digging experience, otherwise a donation is appreciated for a short visit

Hours: variable—call ahead

Best time to visit: anytime, except when it snows

Camping/Lodging: developed camping and lodging in Flagstaff

Access: very easy

Jon's Rating: ★★★★☆ (archaeology)

Jon's Notes:
Although not as well known as other sites of its kind, Elden Pueblo is just as important in its own right. It was likely one of the primary villages of the Sinagua culture from about AD 1150–1275. The main structure is a 60-room pueblo constructed of volcanic rock (plenty of that around here!) that sits atop a much older pit house village. In the summer, the site serves as a hands-on archaeological summer camp for school kids hosted by the Museum of Northern Arizona (right there in Flagstaff). It also caters to families and individuals that wish to experience something of the thrill and tedium of archaeological excavation. Call for information on this unique participatory experience.

LEFT: Ongoing excavations have exposed many of the pueblo walls.

Artwork by Vernon Morris

The sky is falling! OK, not really, just a piece of it. The Winona Meteorite crashes the party at Elden Pueblo 800 years ago.

The Gods Must Be Crazy

In 1928, excavators of the site discovered a small, curious rock carefully buried in a stone cyst within the pueblo walls. Circumstances of the burial suggest the pueblo inhabitants treated this specimen as sacred. As it turns out, the item in question was a section of a small meteor (the Winona Meteorite) that apparently fell during the occupation of Elden Pueblo. Researchers consider it reasonable to speculate some of the pueblo inhabitants may have actually witnessed the meteor's fall, after which they enshrined it as a sacred object. Why this hasn't been reported by tabloids like Weekly World News or National Enquirer is anyone's guess. It certainly merits at least some recognition next to Bat Boy and the Elvis statue on Mars.

Metate grindstone at Elden Pueblo.

Excavations are open to public participation. The whole family can dig it!

FISHERMAN GEOGLYPH

15

Directions:
From Quartzsite, head north on Rt. 95 for 5½ miles. Shortly after mile marker 114, turn east on Plomosa Rd. Follow for about 7¾ miles. Look for a sign just after the wash that announces "Scenic View Parking" directing you into a gravel parking area on left (north) side of road. Follow the dirt track from the parking area for an easy ¼ mile to the outer fence and a brass plaque.

Contact Info:
Arizona BLM office
928-317-3200 or 602-417-9200
www.blm.gov/az/st/en/prog/cultural/fisherman.html

Fee: free

Hours: daylight hours

Best time to visit: anytime; avoid midsummer heat

Camping/Lodging:
basic camping on BLM land nearby; lodging in Quartzsite

Access: easy ½-mile round-trip hike

Jon's Rating: ★★★★☆ (archaeology)

Jon's Notes:
One of the rarest types of sites in Arizona archaeology is the geoglyph, where ancient cultures arranged rocks—or in this case removed rocks— from the surrounding landscape to create particular patterns, shapes, or images. These sites are generally very large scale and often are recognizable only from the air (and then only if some yahoos haven't destroyed the rock arrangement with their off-road ATVs and drunken antics). This one, however, is comparatively small—only about 75 feet long—allowing you to appreciate the site from the relatively safe height of, say, 5 or 6 feet. One visit and you'll understand why space alien cults the world-over embrace these sites as proof-positive of visits from another world. The Fisherman Intaglio is the only such site publicly accessible in Arizona and it's worth the visit even without your own flying saucer.

LEFT: The "Quartzsite Rocks" are nearby the Fisherman Geoglyph and are effectively the lithologic reverse.

RIGHT: Although the images are very subtle, they are easily recognized once you have an idea of the overall composition and orientation. Full length of the geoglyph is about 80 feet from the lower fish to the sun figure.

ABOVE: The "Fisherman".

BELOW: Bigger of the two fish.

Quartzsite Rocks!

Another interesting spot nearby is known locally as "The Quartzsite Rocks" which is, effectively, the lithologic inverse of the Fisherman Geoglyph. Not to be outdone by the natives who preceded them, local white settlers of the area embarked on their own hard-rock expression and piled rock from the landscape into recognizable letters spelling Q-U-A-R-T-Z-S-I-T-E. It's worth seeing because of its contrast to the Fisherman site that was formed in a more subtle way by removing rocks from the desert pavement to make an indented image. To reach the Quartzsite Rocks, travel from the Fisherman parking area back west about 1⅓ miles to a gravel road which branches off to the right (north). Follow this about ³⁄₁₀ mile to a left turn which leads to a wire fence surrounding the rocks.

Beware of these guys! Despite their cute name—Teddy Bear Cholla—they'll cause you a world of hurt if you get too close.

GILA BOX RIPARIAN NATIONAL CONSERVATION AREA

16

Directions:
From intersection of Rt. 70 and 191 in Safford, follow Rt. 70 east 5 miles to Sanchez Rd. Start clocking mileage here. Turn north (left) onto Sanchez Rd. and cross over the Gila River. In about a mile Airport Rd. branches off to the left while Sanchez Rd. bends east. (Stay on Sanchez road.) The pavement becomes intermittent starting at about 7½ miles. At 7¾ miles bear left at the fork. At 9⅓ miles you'll be at the West Entrance kiosk, with signage, a map of the area and a nice overlook of the Gila River.

Contact Info:
BLM Safford office
928-348-4400
www.blm.gov/az/st/en/prog/blm_special_areas/ncarea/gbox.html

Fee: free to visit; fees for camping and river floating

Hours: daily

Best time to visit: anytime

Camping/Lodging: basic camping only; lodging in Safford

Access: most of the roads in the area are rugged and require high-clearance vehicles and often four-wheel drive; always, be careful of flash floods; in addition, hiking in this area is moderate to very difficult

Jon's Rating: ★★★✬☆ (geology)
★★★★☆ (archaeology)

Jon's Notes:
What is a "riparian" anyway? The term refers to environments that occur along the shores of permanent flowing waterways. The "box" idea is a label placed by cartographers on some canyons, which appear "box-like." In this case, a 23-mile segment along the Gila River—including Gila Box itself—and 15 miles along Bonita Creek are included in this special natural conservation area. The whole area is very picturesque and a drive through part of this region is well worth the time. There are several great overlooks and picnic areas. If you have a boat or canoe/kayak, so much the better. Cliff dwellings, rock art and homestead cabins occur along the waterway. Hiking is also popular although it's more difficult to access the ruins in this way. Be aware of flash flood potential any time rain is predicted.

LEFT: Is it a box, or a riparian? Hooray—it's both!

The drive through Gila Box Riparian is scenic and colorful. But don't bother asking locals in Safford about it—for the most part they know very little about this treasure in their back yard.

The Mother Lode

Just north of the Gila Box Riparian NCA is a gigantic hole in the ground which wasn't caused by a meteor impact such as was Meteor Crater. Rather this particular crustal cavity is the result of industrious…, well, industrialists. The demand for copper is huge—the average U.S. home contains over 400 pounds of the near-precious metal and the Phelps Dodge Mining Company has come to the rescue here in a big way. It happens that their Morenci Mine is North America's leading producer of copper and one of the largest open-pit mines in the world—and it looks it! But before you decry blighting of the landscape and destruction of the environment, you should know this facility is a "zero-discharge" operation where no pollutants enter the local watershed. That's good news because Gila Box is just downstream.

View from the overlook at the West Entrance.

Strange but true plants, like this Ocotillo, are abundant here.

GRAND CANYON CAVERNS

17

Directions:
Located on historic Rt. 66 about 25 miles northwest of Seligman.

Contact Info:
Visitor information
928-422-3223
www.gccaverns.com

Fee: per person or group tour fee

Hours: summer: 9–5; winter: 10–5; closed Christmas Day

Best time to visit: anytime

Camping/Lodging: campground and motel on site

Access: easy

Jon's Rating: ★★★☆☆ (geology)

Jon's Notes:
Grand Canyon Caverns has been valiantly clinging to a doomed business plan ever since old Rt. 66 went the way of the dinosaurs. Let's face it—tempting tourists away from the Grand Canyon to see a different sort of hole in the ground that is tiny by comparison and not nearly as colorful is tough business. But they make the most of it with a jovial atmosphere that keeps the "Get your kicks on Rt. 66" spirit

alive. And besides, there's an elevator that takes you down the 210 feet below ground in style. Heck, the Canyon itself doesn't even have an escalator. Don't miss the giant ground sloth! If you're on your way to Havasu Canyon this is the place to stop and refresh.

Cave "flowers" in bloom.

LEFT: It's deep, it's naturally air-conditioned and it's well-lit. What else do you want... an elevator? OK—they've got that too!

Walt's hole in the ground is really big!

Let's add a little color to this scenario.

All That Glitters...

In 1927, a local wood cutter named Walter Peck was on his way to play a game of poker when he stumbled and nearly fell into a large hole. Being the inquisitive type, the next day Walt rounded up some pals and had them lower him into the pit. What he saw astounded him—shiny yellow crystals shimmered in the amber glow of his oil lamp— "GOLD!" he exclaimed to himself. He quickly hatched a plan to buy the land without revealing the treasure he had discovered. While negotiating the land purchase, he gathered ore samples and sent them quietly off to a distant assay office. Finally Walter's ship came in—he succeeded in buying the land and proceeded to develop plans for his mine. It was only after all this that the assay came back effectively torpedoing Walt's ideas—there was no gold, only calcium and iron oxide (rust). But true entrepreneurs always bounce back and Walter Peck then started charging people 25 cents to see his hole in the ground. The rest, as they say, is history.

Who'd have guessed there was a giant hole below this desert?

GRAND CANYON NATIONAL PARK

18

Directions:
From Williams, travel north on Arizona 64 for 55 miles to south entrance. From Flagstaff, follow U.S. 180 north for 82 miles.

Contact Info:
National Park Service
Visitor information
928-638-7888
www.nps.gov/grca

Fee: vehicle entrance fee

Hours: daily

Best time to visit:
North Rim closes in mid-winter due to snow; South Rim is open year-round

Camping/Lodging:
several developed campgrounds and lodges located within the park

Access: easy to extreme

Jon's Rating: ★★★★★ (geology)
★★★✫★ (archaeology)
★★★★★ (paleontology)
★★★★✫ (museum)

Jon's Notes:
You've heard it before—"Grand Canyon is the most incredible, most spectacular, most fantastic, most... etc, etc, etc." Well, it's all true and if you've not been here, you ain't seen nothin' yet! It is one of the seven natural wonders of the world and among Earth's most striking natural features. The Canyon (with a capital C, of course!) is not that old, geologically speaking, having formed mostly as a result of erosion within the last 6–8 million years (that's in the wink of a geologic eye).

There are 3 primary ways to explore the Canyon: by car driving along the rim with its spectacular overlooks, by foot hiking into the back-country and inner canyon, or by the ever-popular rafting expeditions where the phrase "wet and wild" was coined. Another, less tactile, but quite exhilarating method is by hiring onto one of the many small planes or helicopters licensed to fly into the Canyon. Such a flight is truly an IMAX experience but, at the same time, a real annoyance to those on the ground. Somehow the screeching of airplane engines just doesn't jive with the panoramic grandeur of the place.

LEFT: One of the seven wonders of the natural world.

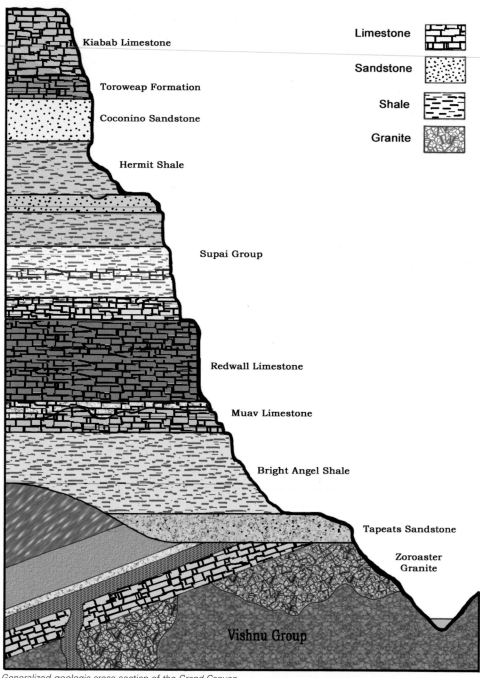

Kiabab Limestone

Toroweap Formation

Coconino Sandstone

Hermit Shale

Supai Group

Redwall Limestone

Muav Limestone

Bright Angel Shale

Tapeats Sandstone

Zoroaster Granite

Vishnu Group

Limestone

Sandstone

Shale

Granite

Generalized geologic cross section of the Grand Canyon.

Permian Lizard Land

The geography of the Canyon is manifestly self-evident. The oldest rocks, the Vishnu Group at the bottom of the inner gorge, are over 2 billion years old while the top—the Kaibab Limestone (look for fossils in this ancient coral reef, they're right under your feet!)—is a mere 260 million. Paleontology plays an important role here as well. The tan-colored cliffs of the upper Canyon walls are Coconino Sandstone which at one time represented a vast sand dune environment (think Sahara Desert). During the Permian Period the area was populated by early mammal-like reptiles which roamed in large groups and whose footprints are exposed in the Canyon 280 million years later. We even find "fossilized raindrops" from that time preserved in the fine sandstone.

Fossil footprints of mammal-like reptiles are found in the Coconino Sandstone of the Grand Canyon. Laoporus, *as depicted here, lived 280 million years ago among sand dunes that covered much of the region at that time.*
(Artwork by Vernon Morris)

Tusayan Ruin is located right along the South Rim Drive.

Fiddling With Twigs

Archaeological sites abound throughout the Canyon but most are remote and difficult to access. One notable exception is Tusayan Ruin, a modest structure of 15 rooms which was occupied briefly from about AD 1185–1225. It's right along the South Rim drive and very easy to access. Next to it is the Tusayan Museum which houses some of the Canyon's artifact collection. Most interesting among the finds are the "split-twig" figures that were found in caves within the park. Over 4000 years old, they represent the oldest record of human occupancy of the Grand Canyon. Some of these effigies appear to be that of bighorn sheep while others may be mule deer. Both of these animals are still very common in the Canyon today. The people that made these little figures were part of what is locally known as the Desert Culture. Their relationship to modern native cultures is uncertain.

Twig figures from caves in the Canyon are 4000 years old. They can be seen at the Tusayan Museum.

GRAND FALLS OF THE LITTLE COLORADO

19

Directions:
Head east from Flagstaff on I-40 about 14 miles to Winona exit. Turn left and follow paved road 2 miles northwest to right on Leupp Rd. Take Leupp Rd. northeast for about 13 miles until you reach a point between 2 cinder cones after which is a sign leading you off the pavement to a dirt road on the left. Follow this track (usually passable by car) 10 miles north to the picnic area and short trail to overlook.

Contact Info:
Flagstaff Visitor Center
800-842-7293
http://navajonationparks.org/htm/littlecolorado.htm

Fee: free

Hours: daylight hours

Best time to visit:
during spring runoff or in the summer after a nice heavy rain

Camping/Lodging: none nearby; both in Flagstaff area

Access:
car access can be difficult in bad weather; falls overlook is easily accessed once at the parking area

Jon's Rating: ★★★★☆ (geology)

Jon's Notes:
The falls are indeed grand if they are working, which most of the year they are not, at least not very well. The Little Colorado is one of many minor tributaries of the mighty Colorado of Grand Canyon fame and, by and large, is not comparable to it. For most of the year, it's a small-to-nonexistent creek with barely anything tracing its course and little coming over the cliff. But in the spring runoff and during summer rain showers, the 185-foot-high falls come into their own, forming an impressive and picturesque sight. Best months are usually March and April. Check with the visitor center in Flagstaff before making the long drive out.

LEFT: Now you know why the locals call this place "Chocolate Falls".

HAVASU CANYON

20

Directions:
Follow Rt. 66 northwest out of Seligman. In 25 miles, stop off at Grand Canyon Caverns for refreshments and gas (you'll be glad you did!). Continue on Rt. 66 for 5 miles to right turn onto Reservation Rt. 18. Follow this 60 miles to Hualapai Hilltop, the end of the road. From here, hike or ride mules another 8 miles to Supai. Be prepared to be amazed.

Contact Info:
Havasupai Tribe
928-448-2121 or 928-448-2141
www.havasupaitribe.com

Fee:
you must have a reservation and a permit from the Havasupai Tribe before entering

Hours: daily

Best time to visit:
not advisable if rain is predicted; avoid midsummer heat

Camping/Lodging:
basic tent camping and lodging at Supai in the canyon

Access:
very difficult, long 8-mile one-way hike to Supai—it seems a lot longer coming back out!

Jon's Rating: ★★★★★ (geology)

Jon's Notes:
Over 500 years ago, the Havasupai Indians settled in this beautiful valley, which lies just south of Grand Canyon National Park. Havasu Canyon is picture-perfect, known for its aqua-blue travertine pools and splendid waterfalls. Thankfully, no roads enter the canyon itself but you are welcome to travel into it from the parking area by mule, horse or on foot, so long as you have made arrangements for lodging or camping beforehand. The 8-mile one-way trek isn't easy, especially if you're hiking, but the rewards are many upon reaching Supai, the settlement at the bottom. The Havasupai are friendly and accommodating, and the setting is unlike any other place on Earth. Plan to spend a few nights—not just one—as the trek in and out takes up too much of your time and you'll want to relax and enjoy all this place has to offer.

*LEFT: Is Havasu Canyon really as fantastic as it looks here? No, it's not—it's **better**!*

In this particular adventure scenario, the best part is the journey AND the destination.

The Unnatural State of Farming

The Havasupai, like the rest of the Indians across North America, have their own story of woe to tell as a result of white expansionism. They once occupied much of the western end of the Grand Canyon, which, as fate would have it, was the first place along the rim that white people chose to settle. Eventually the settlers forced out the Indians who had centuries-old communities atop the Canyon plateau but tolerated their farming along the lower slopes in places such as Indian Gardens along Bright Angel Trail. That, of course, didn't last either. When Uncle Sam created Grand Canyon National Park, the master planners eventually decided native agriculture didn't fit their plans for a natural park. So they kicked the Havasupai farmers out and brought in the railroad with loads more white people. Progress!

Set in a land of natural splandor, the falls of Havasu Canyon are legendary and breathtaking.

HIEROGLYPHIC CANYON

21

Directions:
From intersection of Hwy. 88 in Apache Junction, follow Hwy. 60 east 7 miles to north on Kings Ranch Rd. Turn north on Kings Ranch Rd. and follow 2¾ miles to Baseline. Turn east on Baseline and follow ¼ mile to Mohican. Turn north and follow ⅓ mile to west on Valleyview Rd. and follow (it turns north and becomes Whitetail Rd.) for 1⅓ miles. At the intersection of Whitetail Rd. and Cloudview Rd, turn east and follow ⅓ miles to the end at parking lot. Continue on foot, moderate 1⅔-mile (one way) hike into Hieroglyphic Canyon.

Contact Info:
Tonto National Forest
602-225-5200
www.fs.fed.us/r3/tonto

Fee: free

Hours: daily

Best time to visit: anytime; avoid midsummer heat

Camping/Lodging:
basic camping nearby on Tonto National Forest land; lodging in Apache Junction

Access: moderate to difficult

Jon's Rating: ★★★☆☆ (archaeology)

Jon's Notes:
The ancients knew a good thing when they saw it and a permanent water supply in an arid desert was at the top of their list. Rock art is often associated with such a place and the scenic pools of

Hieroglyphic Canyon are the setting for the petroglyphs that abide here. Unfortunately, as is often the case at rock art sites, modern morons decided to express their towering stupidity by chiseling their own graffiti, often in the same spot. Still, many of the images are fairly clear and the pools themselves, when clean, are picturesque.

LEFT and ABOVE: The Superstition Mountains hold more treasures than just gold, even if the sign maker can't spell.

Lots of cactus, lots of rocks. But lots of petroglyphs, too!

The Dutchman May Be Lost, But Hopefully You Aren't

Over the years there's been a great amount of hoopla over the reputed Lost Dutchman Mine. Legend has it that in the 1870's a gold prospector—Jacob Waltz, the Dutchman as it were (he was actually from Germany, but that's close enough)—had successfully found a hidden gold mine in the Superstition Mountains which supposedly was lost after the original miners—the Peralta family of northern Mexico—had been killed off by Apaches in the 1840's. He apparently worked hard on his mysterious claim for countless years under the secrecy which often accompanies such finds. Curiously, he stashed all the gold and never brought it to town. Well, don't ya know old Jacob finally croaked. He died in 1891 but not before describing to a good Samaritan neighbor the treasure he had secreted away in the mountains. Since that time, countless thousands have searched in vain for the Lost Dutchman Mine. But no one has ever come home with the bacon. The point is, maybe you'll stumble upon it. If you do, please forward us a very reasonable 10% "finders fee" for steering you in the right direction. Thank you.

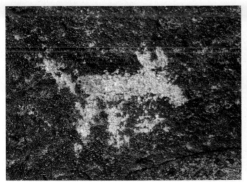 

There's a lot of superstition in the Superstition Mountains. There's also some cool rock art.

HOMOL'OVI RUINS

22

Directions:
From Winslow, head east on I-40 for 4 miles to exit 257. Head north on Arizona 87 about 1⅓ miles to park entrance.

Contact Info:
State Park information
928-289-4106
AZstateparks.com/parks/parkhtml/homolovi.html

Fee: per person or group entrance fee

Hours: daylight hours

Best time to visit: anytime; avoid midsummer heat

Camping/Lodging:
developed campground within park; lodging at Winslow

Access: easy—most trails are paved or maintained

Jon's Rating: ★★★★⯪ (archaeology)

Jon's Notes:
The term Homol'ovi is an Indian term that means "the place of the little hills" and there certainly are an abundance of those in this area around Winslow. The most popular, of course, is the Homol'ovi Ruins State Park, home to more than 300 different archaeological sites and four major pueblos, which thrived here in the 13th and 14th centuries. The Hopi believe that Homol'ovi was a stopping-off point for their ancestors (the Hisatsinom) while they migrated to their present-day home on Black Mesa from the south. They consider the area sacred and some Hopi still come here to remember their ancestors and the journey they made.

LEFT: Homol'ovi I has several dwellings built into sandstone walls, like wannabe cliff dwellings.

Homol'ovi II has struc-
tures built above
ground on a small hill
overlooking the entire
area. Pottery shards
(right) with interesting
patterns abound in the
area, but please leave
them where they are.

A New Park

Homol'ovi is a relatively recent addition to the public trust, becoming a state park in 1991. The park is roughly divided between the two major groups of sites—Homol'ovi I and Homol'ovi II—with a scattering of petroglyph sites in between. Be sure to stop at the great visitor center first for an overview, lest you miss some of the more interesting aspects of this park.

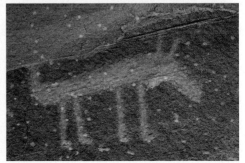

Watch your step in the summertime! Lucky for you there are more Sonoran gopher snake (like this one) than "rattlers."

Some excellent petroglyphs can be found near the ruins at Homol'ovi II.

KARTCHNER CAVERNS

23

Directions:
From I-10 near Benson, follow Hwy. 90 south 9 miles to entrance and get down underground.

Contact Info:
State Park information
520-586-CAVE (2283)
www.azstateparks.com/parks/parkhtml/kartchner.html

Fee: per person or group tour fee

Hours: 7:30am–6pm

Best time to visit: anytime

Camping/Lodging:
superb developed campground on site; nearest lodging is in Benson

Access:
easy, however reservations are highly recommended, especially on weekends

Jon's Rating: ★★★★★⯪ (geology)

Jon's Notes:
This is the crown jewel of the North American underground. In November 1974, two young cavers (real cavers in America do not use the term "spelunking"), Gary Tenen and Randy Tufts, were exploring the limestone hills at the base of the Whetstone Mountains. In the bottom of a sinkhole, they found a narrow crack leading into the hillside. Warm, moist air flowed out, signaling the existence of a cave. After several hours of crawling, they entered a pristine cavern—not just any cavern but what would soon be recognized as one of the finest in the world. For years, the two kept their discovery a secret. It wasn't until February 1978 that they told the property owners, James and Lois Kartchner, about their amazing discovery and urged them to seek protection for it. The cave's existence became public knowledge in 1988 when its purchase was approved as an Arizona State Park. If there is only one cave in the world you visit, make it this one!

LEFT: The jewel of the North America's underground.

Spectacular and nearly-virgin cave formations make this the best underground experience you'll ever see in Arizona and one of the top in the world. Hanging cave "bacon" (above) and pristine soda straw formations (right) along one of the main tour routes. Kartchner has some of the longest soda straw stalactites in the world.

Cave Conservation

Extraordinary precautions have been taken during the development of Kartchner Caverns to conserve the cave's pristine condition, making it perhaps the most well-preserved commercial cavern in the world. Since its discovery, access has been very tightly regulated. In the early days, many would-be explorers—including several bonafide cave researchers—were not allowed. Construction of the public-access areas was stringently controlled to minimize impact on the fragile cave environment. The use of air-locks and close monitoring of its vital signs ensure continued health of the cave environment. The Great Room, for example, is closed mid-April to mid-October during the time it is inhabited by 1000 female Myotis bats. Ongoing geologic, archaeologic and paleontologic research has recorded some 200,000 years of the cave's history.

Get down! It's not hard to get to and easy to tour.

KEYHOLE SINK

24

Directions:
From Williams, take I-40 east to the Pitman Valley exit #171. Turn left and cross over the Interstate. Proceed east on Historic Rt. 66 (Co. Rt. 146) for about 2 miles to the Oak Hill Snowplay Area. Park in this lot. The trail is just across the parking area on the north side of the road.

Contact Info:
Kaibab National Forest/USFS Williams office
928-635-8200
www.fs.fed.us/r3/kai/oldrec/trwc_keyh.html

Fee: free

Hours: daily

Best time to visit: anytime, but not during wet or snowy weather

Camping/Lodging:
basic camping nearby on Kaibab Forest land; developed camping and lodging in Williams.

Access: easy 1½-mile round-trip hike

Jon's Rating: ★☆☆☆☆ (archaeology)
★★☆☆☆ (geology)

Jon's Notes:
This short hike (less than 2 miles round-trip) is easily accessed from Williams but the site itself is likely to let you down if you're hoping

for an archaeological epiphany. Still, it is a pleasant stroll through the pine forest to see a nice example of a basalt "sink" tucked away in a small box canyon. The petroglyph images, such as they are, will be found on the far left side. They're faint and abstract and are thought to be about 1,000 years old.

As in many other important water stations, native cultures inscribed petroglyphs along the walls of the sink.

LEFT: What was once an ancient lava flow became a local water source for natives and white pioneers.

KINISHBA RUINS

25

Directions:
Head to Fort Apache Historic Park by traveling Arizona Rt. 73, from either Pinetop or Carrizo Junction, to its intersection with Indian Rt. 46, about 5 miles south of Whiteriver. Signs at the intersection guide you east to the park where you check in.

Contact Info:
Fort Apache Indian Reservation
Apache Cultural Center
928-338-4625
www.nps.gov/nr/travel/amsw/sw12.htm

Fee: per person or group entrance fee

Hours: Mon–Fri: 8am–5pm

Best time to visit: anytime

Camping/Lodging: camping and lodging nearby in Whiteriver

Access:
easy, but you must access the ruins via a visit to the Fort Apache Cultural Center first

Jon's Rating: ★★★✭☆ (archaeology)

Jon's Notes:
One of the more important Mogollon culture sites, this large, multi-story pueblo had over 400 ground-floor rooms, several two-story and even some three-story ones. Its location at the head of a fertile valley ensured good farmland for the inhabitants. Kinishba was active between AD 1250–1350 and likely housed over 1,000 occupants at the peak of its growth. It, like many other contemporary communities, was inexplicably abandoned early in the 15th century, possibly due to drought and overuse of the nearby arable lands.

LEFT: Twice constructed, twice ruins.

The main structure was restored in the 1930s by Byron Cummings.

Reruined Ruin

Kinishba was excavated and partially restored in the 1930s by Byron Cummings, the great southwestern archaeologist who envisioned a tourist-based education complex here. By the looks of it, Cummings did an incredible job in bringing the site back to life. But things rarely work out as planned and, unfortunately, Cummings's dream was one of those that went south. After ol' Byron signed out of Earth's logbook, the place fell into disrepair and it now looks well on its way to becoming a re-ruined ruin. The most well-maintained aspect of the site seems to be the plaque and stand commemorating Kinishba's inclusion in the National Register of Historic Places, a meaningless designation for a site that is already better protected under state, federal and tribal law.

Sadly, Kinishba is once again on its way to becoming a real ruin.

LAVA RIVER CAVE

26

Directions:
From the intersection of Rt. 180 and Rt. 89 in Flagstaff, drive about 14 miles north on U.S. 180. At milepost 230, turn left onto FR 245, which is a dirt road. Continue 3 miles to left on FR 171. Follow 1 mile and turn left onto FR 171B. Parking area is about ⅓ mile. Follow obvious large path about ¼ mile to cave entrance.

Contact Info:
Coconino National Forest/Peaks Ranger Station
928-526-0866
www.fs.fed.us/r3/coconino/recreation/peaks/lava-river-cave.shtml

Fee: free

Hours: daily

Best time to visit: anytime, but not during wet or snowy weather

Camping/Lodging:
basic camping nearby on Coconino Forest land; developed camping and lodging in Flagstaff

Access:
drive can be difficult in wet weather; hike down into cave entrance is difficult and requires navigation over boulder piles, but after reaching the bottom most of the rest is moderate

Jon's Rating: ★★★★☆ (geology)

Jon's Notes:
Ever walked inside a lava flow? You should if you haven't, but make it "a tall cold one." Lucky for you, one of the best examples of lava tubes in the U.S. is also big enough to walk upright inside most of its passage. This mile-long tunnel was formed roughly 700,000 years ago by molten rock that erupted from a volcanic vent in nearby Hart Prairie. The top, sides and bottom of the flow cooled and solidified first, after which the inside emptied out like a straw, leaving behind the present cave. Be sure to observe the first rule of caving by bringing 3 sources of light for each person (one of which is a good, strong, hand-held electric lantern). Wear warm clothes as the temperature stays between 35–42 degrees year-round. Gloves and hats are also recommended. Leave Rover and Fluffy in the car.

LEFT: Bring a jacket, a few flashlights, and watch your head when you enter!

ABOVE and RIGHT
TOP: The first 50
yards are rocky and
sloped, requiring
careful negotiation.

RIGHT BOTTOM:
Once inside the belly
of the beast the ceiling
is smooth.

Lava Tubes Down Under

You may not have heard much about the phenomenon of lava tubes, but they are quite common in volcanic areas around the world. In Queensland, Australia, for example, there is a place called Undara which was host to a major volcanic event 190,000 years ago that produced 164 volcanoes and more than 300 lava tubes. Only 9 of the tubes have been explored in any length. Some of them are quite extensive—one of the longest has been traced for over 100 miles! These natural subterranean channels are home to many critters including Rock Wallabies, close relative of the Kangaroo. Their hardened foot pads allow them the enviable capacity to jump and romp around the sharp basaltic rock of these tubes. But what does one do with a landscape rife with volcanoes and pavement-hard rock underlain by countless tubular holes? Make it a tourist destination of course, complete with a Lava Lodge and Lava Tube Tours.

A view from inside one of the great lava tubes in Queensland.

Colorful iron oxides line the walls in this tube Down Under.

LAWS SPRING

27

Directions:
From Williams, drive north on Rt. 64 about 5½ miles to mile marker 191—the Spring Valley Road (County Rt. 141)—and turn right. Follow Rt. 141 for about 5 miles (the pavement ends in a couple miles) and turn left on FR 730. Drive 3 miles and bear left on FR 115. Proceed about 2 miles to left on FR 2030. Follow for a little over ½ mile to the parking area.

Contact Info:
Kaibab National Forest/USFS Williams office
800-863-0546
www.fs.fed.us/r3/kai/oldrec/sites_wc_laws.html

Fee: free

Hours: daily

Best time to visit: anytime, but not during wet or snowy weather

Camping/Lodging:
basic camping nearby on Kaibab Forest land; developed camping and lodging in Williams

Access:
car access can be difficult in bad weather; the ½-mile round-trip hike is moderate

Jon's Rating: ★★★✬☆ (archaeology)

Jon's Info:
Access this site by following a ¼-mile path downhill from the parking area. The small basalt box canyon at the trail end is similar to Keyhole Sink, the primary difference being that there are a lot more fine petroglyphs here, even if many have been defaced by woefully moronic hominids. The best panel, undoubtedly, used to be at the spring itself but has since been mostly obliterated by an admittedly well-executed modern glyph proclaiming this is "Laws Spring." Apparently, there was little "law" to consider when the idiots made this sign. However, some excellent, still-intact petroglyphs can be found along the basalt walls uphill to the right as you approach the spring. They are intermittently scattered along the basalt.

LEFT: Though the petroglyphs immediately adjacent to the spring area itself are ruined, the nearby basalt cliffs yet harbor excellent rock art.

ABOVE: Water quality isn't exactly up to the standards of your typical Club Med health spa.

RIGHT: This panel is typical of the local art.

Petroglyph Lite

It's a curious fact about basalt in many regions that it is usually darker on the outside than inside. This is a result of iron minerals, which accumulate on the outer surfaces over countless millennia. Over time, rainwater coursing through the material leaches out the soluble iron inside and deposits it on the outside as the water evaporates. As this process continues, the rock gradually becomes less dark on the inside, while forming a "desert varnish" over its surface, making it a good medium for petroglyphs.

Thanks to some lithologic moron, there's no longer any question which spring this is.

Animals are fairly scarce in these petroglyphs.

The most common images here are 4-legged something-or-others.

LITTLE BEAR ARCHAEOLOGICAL SITE

28

Directions:
From Springerville, follow U.S. 180 south to Eagar. Turn west on Arizona 260 and follow for 5½ miles. Turn left onto gravel road toward South Fork Campground and X Diamond Ranch. Follow signs to ranch offices and museum.

Contact Info:
X Diamond Ranch info:
928-333-2286
www.XDiamondRanch.com

Fee: per person or group fees

Hours: appointment advised but not required

Best time to visit:
anytime except winter; call for excavation schedule

Camping/Lodging:
camping at South Fork Campground; exceptional lodging at X Diamond Ranch; other lodging at Springerville

Access: easy to moderate

Jon's Rating: ★★★★☆ (archaeology)

Jon's Notes:
The Little Bear Site was occupied between about AD 400–800 and is recognized as one of the few localities of its age with an intact central plaza. It's the largest complex of its kind in the area and was likely a cultural and/or religious center for the region. Half a dozen smaller sites of 2–6 rooms each are scattered within a five-mile radius of Little Bear and may have been subordinate to it. Little Bear is about 25% excavated at present with ongoing work performed mostly by volunteers from the general public—that's you! So enjoy it; you won't find a comparable experience in this type of setting.

LEFT: What are you waiting for? You too can help excavate this place!

Although only about a quarter excavated, the Little Bear site shows remarkable architecture and sophisticated construction from 1200–1600 years ago.

We All Dig Archaeology

The site began operations in 2002 as an open-to-the-public archaeological extension of X Diamond Ranch, a museum and log cabin resort complex along the Little Colorado River. Drop-in visits are welcome but it's advisable to book a reservation in advance to get the most out of your experience. All work is directed and supervised by the staff archaeologist, Charles Rand. Every June there's a National Field School hosted by the site where common, everyday folks can participate in more formal training in the science. The site itself is a short, easy hike from the ranch proper. The rental cabins are high-end, excellently maintained and wonderfully spread out around the grounds. They're available for rent by day or week but are very popular and often booked up. Call well in advance if you're hoping to catch one available for your visit, otherwise camp at South Fork or stay in Springerville.

The ruin walls abide still.

Nearby are abundant petroglyphs.

LYMAN LAKE STATE PARK

29

Directions:
Located 11 miles south of St. Johns on U.S. 180/191. Bring the boat, bring the family, bring your pets and have a blast.

Contact Info:
Lyman Lake State Park
928-337-4441
www.azparks.gov/Parks/parkhtml/lyman.html

Fee: per person or group day use and camping fees

Hours: daily

Best time to visit:
anytime, but summer is best with a host of water activities to cool you off

Camping/Lodging: camping, cabins and—for the adventurous—yurts

Access: easy to difficult

Jon's Rating: ★★★★⯪ (archaeology)

Jon's Notes:
Want to hike with the kids to see ancient petroglyphs in the morning and go water skiing in the afternoon? This is the place and, unlike many other Arizona lakes, there's no size restrictions on motorboats. The quiet archaeological aspects of this lake center around two petroglyph trails and two pueblos. The Peninsula Petroglyph Trail is a ½-mile round-trip, self-guided moderate hike accessible across from the campground. It is loaded with excellent, deeply-incised images. The aptly-named Ultimate Rock Petroglyph Trail is a somewhat difficult 1½-mile round-trip hike over much steeper terrain. It has the unique aspect of being accessible only by boat, and then only if there is enough water in the lake. But it's worth it as Ultimate Rock has some of the finest, most unique petroglyphs in the state. Tours to Ultimate Rock are available through the Ranger Station on a seasonal basis. With its variety of great sites and other, more typical state park activities, Lyman Lake is an excellent place to introduce family and friends to the science of archaeology. The only real question remaining is—where did they get the idea for those yurts?

LEFT: Even though the ancients didn't have a lake to water ski on, they still enjoyed living here.

The Peninsula Petroglyph Trail has hundreds of deep, excellent petroglyphs.

All This and Pueblos Too!

If the excellent petroglyphs aren't enough, be sure also to include a stop at Rattlesnake Point Pueblo and Baca Pueblo just 100 yards away from the gravel parking area nearby them. They are accessed via a gravel road that runs south along the lake (ask at the ranger station). In the summer months, rangers lead tours of the sites on weekends and sometimes during the week. Rattlesnake Pueblo was a single-story structure of 80–90 rooms that housed upward of 15 families. Baca was about 70 rooms and housed perhaps a dozen families. Both were active communities between AD 1325–1390. At Baca look for the ledge that has 22 metates in a row!

Rattlesnake Pueblo. We didn't see any rattlers.

Next to Rattlesnake Pueblo is Baca Pueblo with 22 metates in a row. These folks liked to grind maize!

Lyman Lake is home
to many colorful plants
and animals.

*RIGHT: painted lady
butterfly*

*BELOW LEFT:
barrel cactus*

*BELOW RIGHT:
Sonoran gopher snake*

METEOR CRATER

Directions:
Located 20 miles west of Winslow, off I-40 at exit #233. Look for the humongous hole in the ground.

Contact Info:
Meteor Crater Enterprises
800-289-5898
www.meteorcrater.com

Fee: per person or group entrance fee

Hours: summer: 7am–7pm; winter: 8am–5pm

Best time to visit:
anytime; although summer can be stifling, the visitor center is well air-conditioned

Camping/Lodging:
developed camping nearby; closest lodging at Winslow

Access: easy to moderate

Jon's Rating: ★★★★★ (geology)

Jon's Notes:
Named for the man who first determined the correct nature of this geologic anomaly, the Barringer Meteor Crater is the finest such site on the planet. In 1902, Daniel Barringer, a Philadelphia mining engineer, recognized this was not a volcanic structure like the mountain peaks to the west but actually formed as a result of a meteor impact. The "Big Event" happened roughly 50,000 years ago when a huge nickel-iron mass—the Canyon Diablo Meteor—had a bad day and careened into planet Earth at 40,000 miles per hour. The resulting collision blasted out 175 million tons of rock while carving a hole over 500 feet deep and almost a mile in diameter. (Police at the time were amazed but issued no speeding citations.)

LEFT: Aerial view of Meteor Crater. The Big Event left one helluva hole in the ground.

Ka Boom! The Canyon Diablo Meteor does its thing 50,000 years ago east of Flagstaff.

Artwork by Vernon Morris

Space Aliens Assist Bureau of Standards

The Canyon Diablo Meteor is named—if you can believe this—for Canyon Diablo, the small tributary that runs nearby Meteor Crater. During impact, pieces were scattered for dozens of miles around the hole. An important fact about this space rock is its relatively pure iron composition. When the Bureau of Standards was looking for a standard by which to measure iron deposits they had a slight problem—all of Earth's iron is impure at best and highly oxidized. Because of its purity and relative availability, they chose the Canyon Diablo Meteor as the standard for iron deposits worldwide. It's the only extra-terrestrial unit of measure for an economic ore. The Space Aliens have really helped us out on this one, so cut them a little slack, OK?

The Canyon Diablo Meteor exploded into countless zillions of fragments, some of which weigh several pounds.

MONTEZUMA CASTLE

31

Directions:
About 45 miles south of Flagstaff take exit #289 off I-17. After the two roundabouts in front of the Yavapai Apache Casino, turn left and follow the signs.

Contact Info:
National Park Service
Visitor Information
928-567-3322
www.nps.gov/moca

Fee: per person or group entrance fee

Hours: summer: 8am–6pm; winter: 8am–5pm

Best time to visit:
anytime; there is shade to escape the summer sun

Camping/Lodging:
none at the park; camping at Oak Creek Canyon; lodging at the casino or at Sedona

Access: easy; short ¼-mile paved trail from visitor center

Jon's Rating: ★★★★★ (archaeology)

Jon's Notes:
Gotta love the name: Montezuma Castle. There is no castle and Montezuma was never here. Contrary to some ill-informed white pioneers' popular beliefs, these ruins have nothing whatsoever to do with the 16th century Aztec ruler by the same name. Despite this fact, they are hugely impressive. The primary site, situated on a sheer cliff, is a 20+ room structure five stories tall built by Sinagua Indians in the early 1100s. It's in excellent condition due to the restorative work done since its discovery. Other ruins also dot the nooks and crannies of the eroding limestone wall. While in the area, be sure to visit Montezuma Well—a free bonus for your patronage. Both areas were inexplicably abandoned in the early 1400s, a hundred years before Montezuma himself was born. Too bad for him he never got to see any of it.

LEFT: Montezuma Castle—condos with a view.

Several ruins are scattered among cavities in the cliffs along Beaver Creek.

Safety Last?

The view from the dwellings was, no doubt, superb and spellbinding—and dangerous. Although the main structure had 20 rooms and appears to have been used for family groups, all the reconstructions and models of it show no safety ropes or wood railings along the edges of the various platforms. This would be hard to reconcile with all the little kids running around. Either that or these folks couldn't be bothered with something as trivial as safety measures while living 60 feet up a sheer cliff. Maybe the Darwin Awards had some contenders at that time.

One of the most easily recognizable ruins in the Southwest, Montezuma Castle has yielded much in the way of artifacts and information about the Sinagua culture who lived here.

MONTEZUMA WELL

32

Directions:
About 40 miles south of Flagstaff, take exit #293 off I-17 and head east. Drive through McGuireville. Follow Beaver Creek Rd. for another 3 miles and signs to entrance.

Contact Info:
National Park Service
Visitor Information
928-567-3322
www.nps.gov/moca

Fee: free

Hours: summer: 8am–6pm; winter: 8am–5pm

Best time to visit: avoid during midsummer heat

Camping/Lodging:
none at the park; developed camping at Beaver Creek; lodging at Sedona

Access:
easy to moderate; easy paved loop around well; moderate trail to see ruins inside

Jon's Rating: ★★★★★ (archaeology)
★★★☆☆ (geology)

Jon's Notes:
Not far away from Montezuma Castle, this is a textbook example of a limestone sink whose permanent water supply was the primary interest of the local tribes. No slouches at real estate development, the local Sinagua culture took full advantage of this idyllic setting 900 years ago and built several rooms-with-a-view along the cliffs overlooking the sinkhole lake. Bringing in groceries and managing the kids was no doubt a chore for these folks as access was via a system of ladders and/or ropes strung along the wall. A misstep could result in a fall of 80 feet or more with pretty slim chances of landing in the water before cracking your skull.

LEFT: The Well is a classic example of a limestone sinkhole.

True, there's plenty of water, but the funny thing is the primary folks who lived here were called Sinagua, which translates from Spanish as "without water." Don't ask...

Need a Drink?

Montezuma would have been proud had he known this place would be named for him. But, as with Montezuma Castle, he was never here. Still, it's a real treat to have your name attached to such an incredible water supply in a parched desert landscape. Ol' Montezuma must surely be smiling down on those original intrepid, if ill-informed, pioneers, not to mention the National Park Service, for honoring him in such a way. The water from the well actually travels underground again, coursing its way through the wall opposite the main overlook. It reappears in the grove of trees beyond the sink and flows into Beaver Creek.

The remains of a pit house nearby indicates the valley near the well had been occupied thousands of years ago.

MONUMENT VALLEY

33

Directions:
Although mostly in Arizona, some of Monument Valley is in Utah. From Kayenta, take Rt. 163 about 22 miles north and across state line to Monument Valley entrance road. Turn east and follow 3½ miles to visitor center. You'll be safely back in Arizona by that time.

Contact Info:
Navajo Parks and Recreation Department
928-871-6647
www.navajonationparks.org

Fee: vehicle entrance fee and/or backcountry per person fees

Hours: daylight hours

Best time to visit:
avoid during midsummer heat and when heavy rain is predicted

Camping/Lodging:
campground near park entrance; lodging just outside

Access:
easy to moderate; you can drive your own vehicle for an easy spin around the valley or take a more rugged jeep tour of the backcountry; there are also horseback trips for something more equestrian

Jon's Rating: ★★★★★ (geology)
★★★★⯪ (archaeology)

Jon's Notes:
Remember those old western films shot in expansive red valleys backdropped by magnificent buttes and craggy pillars reaching for the sky? Well, they were all filmed here, and if they weren't, then they should have been. Monument Valley is one of the most incredible sights in America. Everywhere you stop it's a timeless vista of breathtaking splendor. The erosional geology itself is legendary, with spindly spires hundreds of feet tall and some of the most incredible natural arches and window rocks you'll ever see. There are also several ruins thousands of years old and plenty of petroglyph panels. As incredible as the self-guided drive is, the best of Monument Valley is experienced only on a backcountry tour. If you have the time, don't even think of leaving here without taking one!

LEFT: There's a whole lot of geology going on at Monument Valley.

The Valley is host to several "Eye" and "Window" rocks, the result of weathering of softer sediments that were surrounded by harder matrix.

Now You See It, Now You Don't

Believe it or not there's a fairly simple explanation for all the ins and outs of Monument Valley. In geologic jargon it's called "selective weathering" which pretty much means what it says. The dramatic lithology of the Valley has been created as a result of erosion which attacks the varied rocks at different rates. The spires and buttes form as soft shales of the Cutler Formation erode out from around the harder vertical concentrations of De Chelly sandstone. Reverse the order of the two and you get cavities—the "windows", "eyes" and natural bridges noticeable in the back country. Both the Cutler and De Chelly are Permian age, having formed some 260 million years ago. The Cutler was deposited primarily as muddy shales in a shallow sea while the De Chelly is a result of compacted wind-blown sand dunes.

Monument Valley has some of the oldest petroglyphs in the state.

Selective weathering results in a real photo-op for city folk as well as the rest of us.

RIGHT: Several excellent ruins await your perusal in the back country.

BELOW: At Monument Valley every stop is a photo op.

NAVAJO NATIONAL MONUMENT

34

Directions:
From Kayenta, head southwest on U.S. 160 for 20 miles to north on Arizona 564. Follow for 9 miles to the monument visitor center and the trail to Betatakin.

Contact Info:
National Park Service
Visitor Information
928-672-2700
www.nps.gov/nava

Fee:
no fees at all—not even for camping in the campground; donations appreciated—give generously

Hours: daily 8am–7pm

Best time to visit: anytime, but avoid during heavy snow

Camping/Lodging:
free basic camping in developed campground; closest lodging in Kayenta

Access: easy to very difficult

Jon's Rating: ★★★★★ (archaeology)

Jon's Notes:
This is one of the best archaeology stops in the Southwest. Three excellent ruins are found here. Betatakin, a 135-room cliff dwelling, can be seen from the easy, paved Sandal Trail (one mile round-trip) along the canyon rim behind the visitor center. You can also access it close-up via a moderately strenuous 5-hour (round-trip) ranger-led hike that drops 700 feet to the canyon floor (remember you have to climb back out again!). To see Keet Seel you must first have a backcountry permit to camp overnight and a reservation for the difficult 8-mile one-way ranger-led hike. But if you're game, you'll be rewarded with a personal view of the largest cliff dwelling in Arizona as well as the best rock art in the area. A third site, Inscription House, is not open to the public but you'll have your hands full with the other two anyway.

LEFT: The cliff which houses Betatakin ruin is almost 1000 feet high.

Artwork by Vernon Morris

Keet Seel as it may have looked about 1275 AD. The reason for the tall poles is a mystery.

Cliff Dwellers Extraordinaire

Tree ring dating tells a very accurate story of the main construction here. Although the three sites differ somewhat in details, the gist of the story goes something like this: the valley below Keet Seel was settled by early Indians around AD 950. About AD 1250 major construction of the Keet Seel cliff dwelling commenced. Betatakin followed about 1267. Major surges in development occurred in 1272 and 1275. The cliff folks were fairly prosperous for four or five decades. However, by 1300, for reasons unknown, at both settlements the landlord kicked everyone out and stole away into the night. Declining crop yields may have been the culprit.

Superb examples of ceramics from the ruins are shown at the visitor center.

An old-style mud-and-earth hogan. This spells fun for the kids!

PAINTED ROCKS

35

Directions:
From Gila Bend, follow I-8 west 14 miles to exit #102 at Painted
Rocks Rd. Head north on Painted Rocks Rd. (paved) about 10½ miles
to fork with Rocky Point Rd. (unpaved). Take left fork onto Rocky
Point Rd. Follow for about ½ mile to picnic and parking area.

Contact Info:
BLM Phoenix Field Office
623-580-5500
www.blm.gov/az/st/en/prog/recreation/camping/dev_camps/painted_rock.html

Fee: free

Hours: daily

Best time to visit:
not advisable if rain is predicted; avoid midsummer heat

Camping/Lodging: basic camping on BLM land

Access: easy

Jon's Rating: ★★★★☆ (archaeology)

Jon's Notes:
You never think of state parks being decommissioned but that's
effectively what happened to Painted Rocks State Park in 1989.
The park had two sections, the area here, which includes the Painted
Rocks themselves, and a "Lake Unit" next to Painted Rocks Dam.
The Lake Unit had to be shut down due to unsafe levels of pollutants
in the Gila River (wonder how that happened?), which precipitated
the demise of the state park.
Thankfully, the Bureau of Land
Management has taken over
and this part of the park is still
maintained with camping spots,
picnic tables, a ramada and even
a pit toilet. Hundreds of petroglyphs and some early historic
inscriptions are found here.

LEFT: What was once a state park is no more. But at least the BLM has kept the site open.

The little hill called
Painted Rocks
is loaded with
petroglyphs. You'd
be hard-pressed to
find a single rock
here that doesn't
have an image on it.

What do these strange figures mean?

The question most often asked in reference to rock art is "What the heck do these markings mean, anyhow?" For the most part they 'mean' whatever you want them to. "That's a cop-out," you say? But really it's as good an answer as you're likely to find. Consider this—for the vast majority of rock art we have no real way of figuring them. We can't ask the artists that made them and we have no Rosetta Stone that can be used to decipher their meaning or intent. Besides that, things are often not what they may seem. In Hopi culture, for example, the symbol of a turtle can be used to denote many things, from a single individual to the Earth as a whole. What is apparent is most rock art was made with great care and purpose. It took many hours and, in some cases, very elaborate tools and techniques to execute these mysterious figures. Some plausible reasons the ancients may have spent such efforts include: clan symbols, mythological icons, territorial markings, expressions of a spirit quest, offerings to deities, accounting systems, recording of important events, solar calendars, astronomical observations, communication with other tribes, and just plain old-fashioned doodling.

It's fun to speculate what these images may have meant to the ancients. Was the petroglyph on the right a representation of a lizard, such as this desert iguana which lives here among the rocks?

PALATKI & HONANKI RUINS

36

Directions:
From Sedona, head southwest on U.S. 89A toward Cottonwood for about 10 miles. One-half mile after milepost 365, turn right onto Red Canyon Rd. In 6 miles the road forks, just after the intersection of Boynton Pass Rd. on the right. The right fork leads to Palatki in 2 miles, the left one goes to Honanki in about 4½ miles.

Contact Info:
Coconino National Forest/Red Rock Ranger District
928-282-4119 or 928-282-3854
http://en.wikipedia.org/wiki/Palatki_Heritage_Site

Fee:
no fee to enter site but you must have a Red Rock vehicle pass, which you can purchase here and at other spots in the district

Hours: daily 9:30am–3:30pm; reservations required

Best time to visit:
anytime so long as you have a reservation (which is free); due to the tiny parking area they discourage drop-in traffic

Camping/Lodging: developed camping and lodging at Cottonwood

Access:
road in can be bumpy; hiking is easy to moderate; trails are short

Jon's Rating: ★★★★⯪ (archaeology)

Jon's Notes:
Located about 30 minutes west of Sedona, Palatki has unique cliff dwellings and some of the best pictographs in the region. It's a great compliment to the V-Bar-V petroglyphs located not far away. Palatki was occupied by Sinagua Indians starting about AD 1150 and abandoned around AD 1300, probably due to diminishing permanent water sources. There are several ruins and shelters that have been excavated and some that have not. Most times there are interpreter guides to show you around. The pictographs indicate the site was likely visited on and off for a much longer period before the Sinagua came along, possibly beginning over 3,000 years ago during the Archaic Period. Honanki is just up the road but this is the better of the two if your time is limited.

LEFT: Palatki Ruin sits in an alcove of geologic splendor.

The occupants of Palatki were accomplished artists, painting pictographs along the canyon walls nearby their cliff house (above).

Bet You Didn't Know...

When you get to the main ruins ask the ranger to show you the finger-prints. In some spots of the original walls, there are well-preserved impressions of fingers and hands that pressed in place the clay mortar 700 years ago. If that's not enough fun for you then just look straight up over your head where you'll see what appears to be ripple patterns in the rock roof about 40 feet above. Well, guess what, they are rip-ples—wind-rippled sand, to be exact. The rock here is part of the Supai Group, which formed as wind-blown sand dunes during the Permian Period. In a serendipitous analogy to the preserved fingerprints of ancient people in ruin walls, so too does the Supai occasionally have preserved prints—only these are of small reptiles that lived among the dunes 280 million (that's right—million!) years ago.
You can see examples of them at the Museum of Northern Arizona in Flagstaff and at the Grand Canyon. And you thought it was all so ho-hum....

Both the Palatki and Honanki sites are situated in cliffs of ancient sandstone which has preserved sandstone ripple marks and fossil footprints of reptiles which lived here in the Permian Period some 280 million years ago.

Honanki is also in a wondrous geologic setting.

Although Honanki features its own great pictographs, you cannot approach the site as close as at Palatki, so these photos are likely the best you'll see of it.

PARK OF THE CANALS

37

Directions:
Located in Mesa at 1710 N Horne St, south of McKelleps, north of Brown Rd. and west of Stapley Dr.

Contact Info:
City of Mesa Parks
480-644-2306
www.parkofthecanals.org/

Fee: free

Hours: daylight hours

Best time to visit: anytime

Camping/Lodging: developed camping and lodging in area

Access: easy

Jon's Rating: ★☆☆☆☆ (archaeology)

Jon's Notes:
It might not seem like much but Park of the Canals is a noble effort to preserve something of the extensive canal system built by the Hohokam people who settled this area nearly 2,000 years ago. At the height of their development, about AD 1000, the Hohokam

had canals irrigating over 100,000 acres, which sustained a population of up to 60,000 people, all of whom were desperate for Frostys but had to settle for plain old agua sin gaso instead. Still, the amount of water these folks managed through engineering is mind-boggling.

LEFT: It looks like an abandoned skateboard park, but fill it with water and you've got irrigation for thousands!

PETRIFIED FOREST NATIONAL PARK

38

Directions:
Petrified Forest National Park stretches north and south between Interstate 40 and Highway 180 about 25 miles east of Holbrook.

Contact Info:
National Park Service
Visitor Information
928-524-6228
www.nps.gov/pefo

Fee: vehicle entrance fee

Hours: summer: 7am–7pm; winter: 8am–5pm

Best time to visit: anytime; avoid midday heat in summer

Camping/Lodging:
no lodging or campgrounds; only backcountry wilderness camping; closest lodging in Holbrook

Access:
roads paved; hiking is easy to moderate, unless you hike into the backcountry, which can be extreme

Jon's Rating: ★★★★★ (paleontology)
★★★★☆ (archaeology)
★★★★☆ (geology)

Jon's Notes:
There's nothing on Earth like the Petrified Forest, a place where 200-million-year-old giant Sequoias lay about like so much cordwood. The fossils here are agatized, displaying a rainbow of colors and patterns. Bones of strange reptiles—including early dinosaurs—have also been found in the park and are displayed in the visitor centers at the two entry points. Early human inhabitants lived and worked here, fashioning stone tools from the colorful agatized wood. The primary archaeology sites—Puerco Ruin and Newspaper Rock—occur about halfway through the park drive and include some fine petroglyphs. Bring your binoculars along at both locations for a better view of the fantastic petroglyphs that abide here. To protect the resource, many areas of the park have designated walkways, but at Jasper Point and some other places you are free to roam around at will. Take advantage of it; seeing the huge, colorful logs up close is an experience that delights the child paleontologist within everyone. But keep in mind, collecting the pretty pieces of agate—or anything else here—is strictly prohibited.

LEFT: At many places in the Petrified Forest—such as Jasper Point here—petrified logs are scattered about like so much cordwood.

Agatized logs at the Petrified Forest sometimes reach four feet in diameter.

Paul Bunyan in Arizona

If you're standing in the Petrified Forest, looking at all the giant fossil logs and thinking to yourself "What a magnificent forest once stood here..." you'll be somewhat disappointed to learn it wasn't quite like that. The towering giants that these logs once were 220 million years ago didn't actually grow in this area. They were transported here by either a prehistoric Paul Bunyan or massive floods that swept them away from their stands along mountains many dozens of miles to the west. Tremendous volcanic eruptions—similar to Mt. St. Helens in 1980—uprooted the giants and floods washed them downstream, quickly burying them in the conglomerated outwash of a floodplain. Babe the Blue Ox had little to do except stand idly by, chewing cud.

The trees may have come from somewhere else, but the dinosaurs lived right here. See their bones at the visitor center.

Artwork by Vernon Morris

At Puerco Ruin you'll see some exposed pueblo walls as well s the petroglyph handiwork of the locals who lived there.

Dinosaurs in the Forest

If Paul Bunyan and Babe the Blue Ox spent any time logging here 220 million years ago before they traveled to the North Woods, they no doubt enjoyed the scenery and the variety of animals that were indigenous to the region at the time. Dinosaurs were not uncommon, although they were fairly small by dinosaurian standards. Most were predatory bipedal ornithischians (similar to Coelophysis or Chindesaurus, below) that may have traveled in groups. Others were four-legged armored phytosaurs. Phytosaurs are the most common fossil vertebrate found at Petrified Forest. These animals were very crocodile-like in nature and probably lived in similar ways to them, frequenting streams and rivers of the region in Late Triassic time. They were carnivorous, most likely feeding on fish and smaller reptiles.
Obviously they paid little attention to Paul or Babe.

Artwork by Vernon Morris

Chindesaurus *was a bipedal predatory dinosaur friendly to Paul Bunyan.*

PICTURE ROCKS

39

Directions:
The petroglyphs are located at the the Redemptorist Renewal Center, 7101 W. Picture Rocks Road. From 1-10 in Tucson, take Ina Rd. west about 3 miles. Turn south (left) on Wade Rd. As it curves to your right the name will change to Picture Rocks Road. Proceed another ½ mile to the center, on the left.

Contact Info:
Redemptorist Renewal Center
520-744-3400
www.desertrenewal.org

Fee: no fee but donation appreciated

Hours: daily

Best time to visit: any season during daylight hours

Camping/Lodging:
no camping; rooms available as spiritual retreat for groups or individuals

Access: about as easy as it gets—there's even ecclesiastical support

Jon's Rating: ★★ ☆ ☆ ☆ (archaeology)

Jon's Notes:
Ambling along the trail to Picture Rocks from the retreat center parking area, one can appreciate the reason people of all faiths come here to commune with the spirit world while strolling along ancient pathways contemplating the mysteries of life. But when you get to the petroglyphs themselves you're reminded that even modern humble people of faith can become overly exuberant in displaying their devotion as well as their lack of common sense. A giant cross is planted atop the hill that contains the rock art and, if that wasn't enough, an enormous plaque with a painting of the Madonna is cemented in the hill as if to say "Hey, look at me!" Ironically, at the base of all this is a sign that warns you to "Keep Off the Rocks!"

LEFT: You don't have to travel far from your hotel room for some great ancient culture—there are some excellent petroglyphs right in Tucson!

PUEBLO GRANDE

40

Directions:
The museum is located at 4619 E Washington, just east of 44th St. on the south side of Washington in Phoenix. It's close enough to see the airport from the site but, sorry, you can't claim your baggage here.

Contact Info:
Pueblo Grande Museum
877-706-4408
www.pueblogrande.org/

Fee: fee area Monday–Saturday, but Sunday is free

Hours: Mon–Sat: 9am–5pm; Sun: 1pm–5pm

Best time to visit: anytime

Camping/Lodging: camping and lodging in Phoenix

Access: easy all the way

Jon's Rating: ★★★★☆ (archaeology)

Jon's Notes:
Air travel just isn't what it used to be, is it? But think of the benefits, such as nice, leisurely, unplanned layovers in an overcrowded metro-politan quagmire. Pueblo Grande Ruins is located nearly right off the end of the runway at a 1,500-year-old Hohokam village in the midst of modern day Phoenix. If you have a layover of any length at the airport, you can easily visit this 102-acre park—just grab a cab out front. If you don't want to be taken for a tourist, assume the inflections of native teenage dialect and utter something like "Yo, Bro, you know, let's go to Ho-ho (kam)!" Or, you could simply just ask to be taken to Pueblo Grande like everyone else. Once there, you'll find a huge, football-stadium-sized platform mound that survived largely intact, as well as an excavated ball court, other ruins and a great museum.

LEFT: Martha Stewart herself would be proud of the simple-yet-elegant interior decorating scheme in this 1500-year-old Hohokam hut.

ABOVE:
Reconstructed build-
ings make up the pri-
mary site at Pueblo
Grande.

RIGHT: Some incredi-
ble pottery, such as
this effigy vessel, have
been found here.

(Artwork by Vernon Morris)

Sam Walton's Inspiration?

This site also includes some of the last remaining intact Hohokam irrigation canals and they are impressive. It's a well-known fact the Hohokam were accomplished agricultural engineers. Their irrigation canals were elaborate and very extensive, to the point of being labyrinthian. During its peak in the 1300s, Pueblo Grande was one of the largest settlements in the Phoenix area, encompassing an area of over two square miles. There were several residential communities surrounding a great house much like Casa Grande. No doubt Sam Walton borrowed the idea of this retail development plan from the ancients and parlayed it into the modern Wal-Mart approach. Someone should tip off *Weekly World News* on that one.

If you've got time to kill, or even if you don't, Pueblo Grande is worth a stop.

RAINBOW BRIDGE

41

Directions:
The natural bridge itself is actually in Utah but the easiest access is from Page, via a very scenic 35-mile boat trip that is well worth the price. Several tour companies in Page, as well as Wahweap and Bullfrog Marinas offer day trips to this impressive site.

Contact Info:
Glen Canyon NRA Visitor Center
928-608-6200
www.nps.gov/rabr

Fee:
no fee if you have your own boat—if not, you'll have to pay for a tour and/or guide

Hours: daylight hours

Best time to visit: anytime

Camping/Lodging: camping nearby; lodging in Page

Access:
best access is by boat, which can be hired in Page or Wahweap

Jon's Rating: ★★★★⯨ (geology)

Jon's Notes:
Natural arches are always an awesome sight but this one is the grand-daddy of them all. At 275 feet wide and 290 feet tall, Rainbow Bridge is the largest natural span in the world. Arches hold special meaning for native cultures. Half a dozen Indian tribes consider Rainbow Bridge a sacred place, one that requires respect and reverence. It is deemed very disrespectful and major bad luck to walk under the bridge before paying homage to it through a special native prayer ritual. Since it is unlikely that you know any more about the ritual than the man on the moon, please respect the tradition by NOT walking under it. You can't see it from up close anyway.

LEFT: The Granddaddy of Arches.

ROCK ART RANCH

42

Directions:
Just southeast of Winslow, along Chevelon Creek. Call for directions and to arrange access.

Contact Info:
Rock Art Ranch
928-288-3260
http://anthropology.arizona.edu/rock-art-ranch

Fee: per person or group entrance fee

Hours: daily appointments, but closed Sunday

Best time to visit:
not advisable if rain is predicted; avoid midsummer heat

Camping/Lodging:
basic camping only; closest lodging is in Winslow

Access:
easy car access over maintained dirt and gravel roads; hiking in the canyon is easy to moderate

Jon's Rating: ★★★★☆ (archaeology)

Jon's Notes:
If you were to drive around the state looking for likely rock art sites, you would surely miss one of the most impressive. Rock Art Ranch is situated along Chevelon Creek, a small tributary to the Little Colorado, which has cut a deep hidden canyon into the otherwise flat desert landscape. The walls here are lined with literally thousands of petroglyphs, some of which have, sadly, been recently "repecked" by misguided amateurs. Still, the sheer number of images is overwhelming and many remain in their original condition. It is obvious the area was utilized multiple times over countless years with several generations of petroglyphs inscribed along the canyon. If petroglyphs are your thing, this place is a must-see on your list.

LEFT: The canyon walls at Rock Art Ranch are so rich with petroglyphs you sometimes have trouble sorting them out. There are over a dozen in this photo.

*Chevelon Creek
is home to an
incredible canyon
full of petroglyphs.*

The Management

Your host here is Brantley Baird, a soft-spoken rock art enthusiast who has owned the ranch since the 1940s. He has outfitted the area with an overlook, picnic tables and a very unusual privy. There's a modest entrance fee depending on group size. You are welcome to spend the night so long as you are self sufficient. Mr. Baird also has

a pretty impressive collection of artifacts he and his friends have found on the property, so be sure to ask for a visit to his museum.

All kinds of strange animals and space-alien-like anthropomorphs are found here.

ROMERO RUIN

43

Directions:
From Tucson, drive north on U.S. 77 for about 6 miles after Ina Rd. At milepost 81, turn east into Catalina State Park. Drive to the parking area at Sutherland Wash and follow the Romero Ruin trail for a less than ¾-mile easy hike.

Contact Info:
Catalina State Park
Visitor Information
520-628-5798
http://azstateparks.com/Parks/parkhtml/catalina.html

Fee: per person or group entrance fee to Catalina State Park

Hours: daily 5am–10pm

Best time to visit: anytime

Camping/Lodging: camping nearby; lodging in Tucson

Access:
easy drive; from the parking lot it is a moderate ¾-mile round-trip hike up to the ruin

Jon's Rating: ★★✦☆☆ (archaeology)

Jon's Notes:
The Romero Ruin Interpretive Trail leads from the parking area and eventually meanders through the ruins of a prehistoric Hohokam village site covering 15 acres on a ridge overlooking Sutherland Wash. The hiking is great, the scenery and setting are great and the interpretive signs are great also. What isn't so great is the ruins themselves. Despite the fact that it's one of the largest and most significant archaeological sites within the northern Tucson Basin, Romero Ruin is not a very impressive sight to behold. There really is not much left to see, save the hilltop locality where you get the impression that this would be a great place to camp!

LEFT: Romero Ruin is just one of the wonderful hikes in Catalina State Park.

The setting is nice and the hike isn't long, so just do it.

Rancher Romero

For what it's worth, the ruins are the remains of a Hohokam village that was occupied between AD 500 and 1450. The primary site consists of a perimeter wall, up to six feet high, enclosing a cluster of homes and other buildings. Between about AD 750 and 1000 the inhabitants built two ball courts on the hill. It has been suggested that ceremonies at these courts combined sports and religious functions. The spot is named for rancher Francisco Romero who, during the latter half of the 19th century, built four or five rooms of mud and rock "borrowed" from the abandoned Hohokam village.

Romero Ruin is set among the Catalina Mountains, but you don't have to climb to the top to enjoy the view.

Fishhook cactus in bloom. Look for these in mid to late summer.

SAN PEDRO RIPARIAN NATIONAL CONSERVATION AREA

44

Directions:
There are three main access points to this area, all of which are east of Sierra Vista. To reach the San Pedro House nature center—the main hub for this place—head east on Hwy. 90 about 7 miles. Just before it crosses the San Pedro River, turn right into the parking area. Ask there for directions to Murray Springs Interpretive Trail and Petroglyph Discovery Trail.

Contact Info:
BLM Sierra Vista office
602-417-9200
www.blm.gov/az/st/en/prog/blm_special_areas/ncarea/sprnca.html

Fee: free

Hours: daily

Best time to visit: anytime; avoid during rainstorms

Camping/Lodging:
basic camping only; lodging nearby in Tombstone and Sierra Vista

Access: trails are mostly easy to moderate, especially at San Pedro House; pay attention on the Petroglyph Discovery Trail as the trail to the second petro site is not very well marked

Jon's Rating: ★★★☆☆ (archaeology)

Jon's Notes:
There's that word again—riparian—but since you already picked it up in the listing for Gila Box NCA, we won't bore you with that lesson again. Here a 36-mile segment of San Pedro River north of the Mexico border has been set aside as an area of scientific and environmental interest. All this is especially well presented at the San Pedro House on the south side of the NCA. It has interpretive trails explaining the whole enchilada. There are two primary archaeological sites that warrant consideration, although neither have much left to see other than information stations along walking paths. Both of these sites are the focus of Murray Springs Interpretive Trail, a ½-mile-long presentation of late Pleistocene (Ice Age) life through 10 exhibits along an easy pathway. The San Pedro Riparian NCA also has several petroglyph sites, some of which can be seen along the new Petroglyph Discovery Trail near the Charleston/Millville crossing.

LEFT: It looks quiet enough but this place saw a lot of activity in the prehistoric past.

Artwork by Vernon Morris

"Finally a real meal! I'm sick of those microwave dinners back at the cave..."

Clovis Hunters Bag a Big One

In 1952, a local rancher by the name of Ed Lehner discovered strange bones weathering out of his land along the San Pedro River. He had the presence of mind to call in archaeologists from Arizona State Museum who excavated the skeleton, which turned out to be a mammoth. Not just any mammoth, but one that was killed and butchered by Clovis culture hunters 11,000 years ago. Then, in the late 1960s, University of Arizona excavated another site along the river—the Murray Springs Clovis Site—that included numerous artifacts and bones. These two sites are the ones featured in the Murray Springs Interpretive Trail.

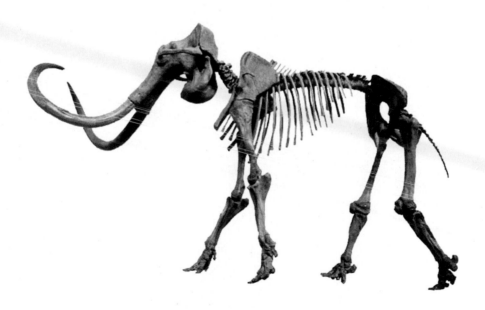

Fire up the barbee, with these ribs we'll eat like kings! Mammoths commonly reached 12 feet tall.

SEARS POINT

45

Directions:
From Gila Bend, follow I-8 west about 37 miles to exit #78 at Spot Rd. Follow north-side service road 1¼ miles east (pavement ends after first ½ mile) to Ave. 76E. Head north, following the main road, which can get a little rough but is generally passable by regular car so long as the weather is dry. In about 6 miles you'll drop down into the Gila River valley. Stay on the main tract which bends west and ends at Sears Point in about 7 miles from the interstate service road. There's signage at this lot.

Contact Info:
BLM State Office
602-417-9200
www.blm.gov/az/st/en/prog/cultural/sears/petro.html

Fee: free

Hours: daylight hours

Best time to visit:
not advisable if rain is predicted; avoid midsummer heat or you'll fry out here

Camping/Lodging: basic camping on BLM land; closest lodging in Gila Bend

Access:
road is maintained dirt and gravel passable by most vehicles most of the time, but it does get bad in wet weather—do not attempt to reach this site in anything but dry weather unless you have 4-wheel drive and high clearance

Jon's Rating: ★★★★☆ (archaeology)

Jon's Notes:
The area of Sears Point has obviously been utilized by different cultures for thousands of years and is rich with archaeological remains. Chief among them are the petroglyphs, which are often very clear and are abundantly scattered among the basalt outcrop. Here you'll find some of the best petroglyph images in the state. There are also other important archaeological features in the area such as rock shelters, "sleeping circles," geoglyphs (images outlined in stone), cairns and unique rock alignments that may constitute astrological sites. This area is very sensitive—please be sure not to disturb any ruin or artifact you may come across.

LEFT: Did the space aliens land here?

ABOVE: Artistic anthropomorphs abide in abundance.

RIGHT: One of the "sleeping circles", although it is doubtful the ancients used it for slumber parties as the name suggests.

Chocolate Frosting

These images are etched into boulders and columns of basalt from an ancient lava flow. You'll notice the old lava forms a protective "cap rock" over the softer sediments below it, giving the area a somewhat butte-like appearance. High iron content of the basalt gives it (and most lavas) a dark coloring from the start. However, weathering elements tend to leach iron minerals from inside the rock and deposit it like paint on the surface, while lightening the inside. This is called desert patina or desert varnish. When the artist pecks below the surface, the lighter contrasting color of the inner rock is revealed and— presto!—a petroglyph is born.

Get your fill of ancient images at Sears Point.

SIGNAL HILL PETROGLYPHS

46

Directions:
From Tucson, go west on Speedway Blvd., which becomes Gates Pass Rd. Turn right at the "T" onto Kinney Rd. Travel 4½ miles to the information center. Signal Hill is 3½ miles farther on Kinney Rd. Weight and length restrictions apply on Gates Pass Rd. RVs should take Ajo Hwy. west from I-19 (exit 99). Turn right on Kinney Rd. and travel 3½ miles to Signal Hill.

Contact Info:
Saguaro National Park/Tucson Mountain District
520-733-5158
www.nps.gov/sagu

Fee: vehicle entrance fee

Hours: daily 9am–5pm

Best time to visit: anytime, but avoid midsummer heat

Camping/Lodging:
no camping or lodging within west part of this park; closest camping is Gilbert Ray Campground in Tucson Mountain Park; closest lodging is in Tucson.

Access:
easy drive; from the parking lot it is a short (¼ mile round-trip), moderate hike up the hill overlooking the picnic area

Jon's Rating: ★★★☆☆ (archaeology)

Jon's Notes:
You've heard the saying "It's the journey, not the destination." That's almost the case here, except the destination is nearly as interesting in a different sort of way. A trip to Signal Hill requires driving through some of the most picturesque desert in North America, the Saguaro National Monument, named for the cactus trademark of the Southwest. There's nothing quite like a Saguaro with their majestic crinkly arms throwing out to the sky. They grow prolifically here forming something of a sci-fi forest. The petroglyphs, on the western side of the park adjacent to a picnic area, include spirals, several animals and abstracts. Although not one of the more famous petroglyph sites, the trip holds a lot of scenic desert pleasure.

LEFT: The drive is only half the fun...

...the other half is the petroglyphs at the end.

Cactus As Culinary Convenience

As with other cactus, the Saguaro have been, and are still today, a source of food to native populations. The fruits of many cactus—especially the Prickly Pear shown here—are not just edible, they are delicious and high in vitamin C. Native cultures harvested cactus fruit when it was in season, much in the same way people do today. The problem the ancients had with collecting cactus fruit is the limited shelf life—once the fruits are removed from the plant they start to sour. If you see ripe fruit, get someone who knows to show you how to extract it safely and taste it right off the plant. Whatever you do, DON'T just grab it—you'll never forget the zillions of microscopic needles that bury into your palm and fester there for weeks. Ripe fruit may be eaten on the spot here, but cannot be collected or removed from this park.

Saguaro cactus in bloom.

Prickly Pears with fruit. Watch those spines!

SLIDE ROCK STATE PARK

47

Directions:
On U.S. 89A, drive 21 miles south from Flagstaff, or 6 miles north from Sedona. You can't miss it. If you do then your in-car GPS has an attitude problem or you've been asleep at the wheel. Either way, you've got a problem.

Contact Info:
Slide Rock State Park
928-282-3034
Water Quality Hotline: 602-542-0202
http://azstateparks.com/Parks/slRO/index.html

Fee: vehicle entrance fee

Hours: summer: 8am–7pm; winter: 8am–5pm

Best time to visit: anytime; especially during hot summer days

Camping/Lodging:
developed camping along Oak Creek Canyon; closest lodging is Sedona

Access: easy to moderate

Jon's Rating: ★★★✦✫ (geology)

Jon's Notes:
Who needs human-made swimming pools when nature can do the act much better? This place is the original water park. Slide Rock is a portion of beautiful Oak Creek Canyon whose red sandstone bed has been worn so smooth it has become a natural water slide. The several slides are punctuated by pools, some of which are actually deep enough for a bona fide swim. Unfortunately, its location downstream from many campgrounds and buildings creates questionable water quality, especially in midsummer. On bad quality days, the watery fun is cancelled, lest you end up with a weird skin rash, intestinal bug, or worse. The good news is the water is tested daily so we recommend you call before your visit.

LEFT: A slot canyon in the making.

Located near Sedona, Slide Rock State Park is in a natural setting unparalleled by even the water parks of Disney World!

Recipe for a Water Park

What would you name the geologic fault running through Oak Creek Canyon? If your answer is Oak Creek Fault, than chalk up 10 points for your superior geologic acuity and continue on with your PhD in the subject. By following the weak, fractured rock that such a fault zone creates, Oak Creek has eroded and enlarged certain fissures to the point where we can enjoy them as a natural water park. The creek will continue its aquatic sculpting so long as there's water flowing. You'll notice that some channels of the waterway are over 12 feet deep yet are only a few feet across. Thus, what you see here is the beginnings of a natural "slot canyon."

Remember when the lifeguards used to tell you not to run around the pool? Same thing applies here. Although the rapids look placid enough, approach the water with caution. If you run up to the creek's edge you're guaranteed to fall right on your butt as soon as your feet touch the slippery algae. But at least you'll no longer wonder why the place is called "Slide Rock".

SOUTH MOUNTAIN PARK

48

Directions:
Located on southern side of Phoenix city limits. Follow Central Ave. south to main entrance and visitor center.

Contact Info:
City of Phoenix
Visitor information
602-262-7393
www.phoenix.gov/parks/trails/locations/south-mountain

Fee: no fees to enter the park at this time

Hours: daylight hours

Best time to visit: anytime, but avoid midsummer heat

Camping/Lodging: camping and lodging in Phoenix

Access: easy to moderately difficult

Jon's Rating: ★★★★☆ (archaeology)

Jon's Notes:
One might think that a community of multiple millions sprawled across very arid desert with a hugely over-extended water supply would cause some sort of self-balancing limitation in population growth. But, hey, this is America and what we wants, we gets! For the last 20 years, Phoenix has consistently been one of the fastest growing cities in the country, complete with golf courses, RV parks and more than one Wal-Mart Supercenter. The morass has enveloped South Mountain Park like a beehive surrounds its queen. But thanks to some forward-thinking city residents in the 1920s, the gem that is

South Mountain Park has been preserved. Hiking here will allow you to breathe freely and forget for a time that you're surrounded by 3½ million people in one of the most congested metropolitan quagmires of the country. All the while, you'll be walking among primal pathways surrounded by some of the best petroglyphs the Southwest has to offer. You may even find yourself conversing with ancient spirits.

LEFT: An oasis in the city.

Concentric circles, spirals, simple and complex geometric shapes abound in South Mountain Park.

Hohokam Artistry

Located south of downtown Phoenix, South Mountain Park is an oasis of nature and of rock art. At 16,500 acres, it is perhaps the largest city park in the world, but that's not the reason to visit. Some of the best and most intriguing petroglyphs you'll ever see are scattered among its peaks and washes. Not only will you find all kinds of bizarre abstract patterns, but you'll also encounter fanciful animal designs, elaborate scenes and unique dancing figures—human forms with one arm raised high and the other on the hip. Most of these images were executed by Hohokam artists AD 750–1400, although some may be much older or younger.

Enjoy a walk in the park—there's 16,500 acres of it!

SUNSET CRATER VOLCANO
NATIONAL MONUMENT

49

Directions:
From Flagstaff, take U.S. 89 north for 12 miles, turn right on the Sunset Crater-Wupatki Loop road and continue 2 miles to the visitor center.

Contact Info:
National Park Service
Visitor Information
928-526-0502
www.nps.gov/sucr

Fee:
per person entrance fee but your pass allows you to also access Wupatki National Monument to the north

Hours: daily 9am–5pm; may be open longer during summer

Best time to visit: anytime; except in snowy weather

Camping/Lodging:
there is a developed campground at Bonito near the west entrance; primitive camping on Coconino Forest lands nearby; closest lodging is Flagstaff

Access: easy to moderate

Jon's Rating: ★★★★☆ (geology)

Jon's Notes:
OK, so it's not Hawaii, but it is closer! At least if you're in Arizona. Sunset Crater is the result of the most recent volcanic activity of the region, having last erupted AD 1064 in a series of events that are considered the only eruptions in the Southwest indisputably witnessed by local peoples. (This, of course, is conjecture based on Hopi legend and some sketchy rock art that may, or may not, depict a volcano erupting and may, or may not, be the one that produced what may, or may not, have been Sunset Crater. The witnesses were unavailable for comment and did not return phone calls to our office.) The fact is, for a time, Hephaestus felt a little agitated and brought the dormant San Francisco Volcanic Field back to life in a big way. When the field again grew quiet, a classic example of a cinder cone, Sunset Crater Volcano, stood 1,000 feet above a dramatically altered land of lava flows and cinders. It's one of the best such examples in North America and is yours to enjoy.

LEFT: It's not Hawaii but it's on your route.

Arizona sponsors a "Shake and Bake" contest 900 years ago.

Artwork by Vernon Morris

Bombs Away!

The Department of Homeland Security may not consider it polite conversation to talk about "bombs" in mixed company, but we're gonna risk it anyway. As is often the case, volcanoes here were sometimes violent, not just spewing off at the mouth and throwing around a few curse words, but unleashing giant explosive events that hurled vile globs of magmatic goo dozens of miles away. To a geologist this means great fun! Albeit 900 years after the fact, the thing we like to do is go looking for those blasted goobers, which we call *volcanic bombs*. Don't know what they look like? Volcanic bombs can be quite interesting. They often have modified tear-drop shapes and show signs of their stratospheric ride in the form of striations, keels and grooves twisted along their surfaces. There are some great examples in the visitor center.

Lookout! It's not just a rock, it's a bomb!

Even in such forbidding environments, some plants find a way to thrive.

TONTO NATIONAL MONUMENT

50

Directions:
From Globe, follow Arizona Rt. 188 northwest 34 miles to Monument entrance. For a real treat, follow the Apache Trail (Arizona Rt. 88) north out of Apache Junction (just east of Phoenix) to the monument. It's one of the most scenic drives in the Southwest. But do it in good weather—the last 22 miles are dirt/gravel with some real cliff-hangers.

Contact Info:
National Park Service
Visitor Information
928-467-2241
www.nps.gov/tont

Fee: per person or group entrance fee

Hours: 8am–5pm; closed Christmas Day

Best time to visit: anytime

Camping/Lodging:
camping nearby at Theodore Roosevelt Lake; lodging in Globe

Access:
hike to Lower Ruin is a 1-mile round-trip moderate trek on paved, but sometimes steep trail; hike to the more impressive Upper Ruin is 3 miles round-trip and is more difficult

Jon's Rating: ★★★★☆ (archaeology)
★★★☆☆ (geology)

Jon's Notes:
Yes, it really is "Tonto" but don't let the name fool you. This monument contains over 70 archaeological sites centered around the Salado Indians, who constructed some important cliff dwellings here about AD 1250–1300. It features three primary sites. The Lower Ruin and Lower Ruin Annex are a short ½-mile (1 mile round-trip) self-guided hike from the visitor center but it can be moderately difficult in hot weather due to the elevation gain. It has 16 ground-level rooms and 3 second-story rooms. Trips to the more impressive Upper Ruin follow a trail that runs along a steep creek bed. It takes 3–4 hours with a ranger and must be reserved in advance. They are offered only in the winter months, November–April. It has 32 ground-level rooms and at least 8 second-story ones.

LEFT: The Ritz circa 1250 AD.

We are pleased to announce our newest rooms come with walk-out verandas and spacious, open floor plans.

The Good Old Days

The oldest permanent dwellings in the Tonto basin date from the second century AD. Communal structures and arrangements of pit houses show evidence of stable farming communities. These villages were apparently abandoned about AD 600. The area was not permanently used again for over 150 years when Hohokam culture people moved in and established their own pit house towns. By AD 1150 there was a fundamental change in pottery styles, construction methods and settlement patterns, which indicated a departure from Hohokam traditions. These changes heralded the emergence of a new culture—the Salado—who were responsible for the cliff dwellings at Tonto.

The Lower Ruin still contains some of the original wood structure from 800 years ago.

TONTO NATURAL BRIDGE STATE PARK

51

Directions:
The park is located off Hwy. 87, about 10 miles north of Payson.

Contact Info:
Tonto Natural Bridge State Park
928-476-4202
www.azparks.gov/Parks/parkhtml/tonto.html

Fee: per person or group entrance fee

Hours: summer: 8am–7pm; winter: 9am–5pm

Best time to visit: anytime

Camping/Lodging:
none on site but several camping areas nearby; lodging in Payson

Access: car access easy; trails are easy to difficult

Jon's Rating: ★★★⯨☆ (geology)

Jon's Notes:
Some people have all the luck! While wandering the area in 1877, David Gowan, a Scottish prospector, was spotted by Apache Indians who apparently had an attitude about explorers and white prospectors in general. Determined to rid the region of this menace, the Indians chased him deep into this particular ravine along the Mogollon Rim. Gowan hid for two nights and three days in one of several caves that dot the inside of this natural travertine bridge. The Apaches, having better things to do, eventually left without finding him. Upon his emergence he was so impressed by the place that he laid claim to it and even persuaded members of his family to emigrate and live there. "What about the Apaches?" you might ask. It seems ol' David forgot all about them, and apparently they did the same with him.

LEFT: Not just another hole-in-the-ground, but an extraordinary place to hide from Indians.

*A travertine hole
that's both picturesque
and serves as a good
hideout, too.*

Erosional Fun

The basis of this giant arch was formed in a collaborative effort by a series of mineral-rich underground springs that built up immense deposits of travertine (calcium carbonate, also called cave onyx) over loads and loads of time. Eventually, Pine Creek, a permanent year-round waterway looking to impress the locals, eroded a hole in the structure and has been widening it ever since. This park features several trails of various lengths from easy to very difficult. Be careful of your footing as the moss, algae and moisture from the falls can make for the proverbial slippery slope.

Some excellent flowers abide here, like these Columbine.

Duck and cover...

TUBA CITY DINOSAUR TRACKS

52

Directions:
From Tuba City, follow U.S. 160 west about 6 miles. Before the intersection with U.S. 89, look for a small, ratty, old wooden sign on the left and a turn-off opposite it on the right. The site is about ¼ mile down this dirt road on the left. You'll see the trinket stands.

Contact Info:
www.experiencehopi.com/dinosaur-tracks.html

Fee: voluntary donation to guide—be generous, they depend on it

Hours: daily

Best time to visit:
anytime; avoid midday heat in summer; it can get ugly during a sandstorm

Camping/Lodging:
closest camping at Navajo National Monument; there are several motels to choose from in Tuba City

Access: as easy as it gets

Jon's Rating: ★★★★☆ (paleontology)
★★★★★ (archaeology)

Jon's Notes:
You simply won't find better "dinosaurian paleoichnofauna" (dinosaur tracks) with this kind of easy access—they are literally right next to the parking area. The variety and good preservation make this one of the best public sites of its kind in the Southwest. The dinosaurs in question lived during the Jurassic Period some 175 million years ago along mud flats that eventually hardened into the rock you see here. Being on the Navajo Reservation you are required to have a guide despite the fact that a) the tracks are nearly visible from the car window, and b) the local "guides", though well-meaning enough, are often confused about what's what in the world of paleontology. The good news is there's no set fee—it's by donation only. By giving up a few bucks you help the local economy and have a unique chance to hang with the homies.

LEFT: Walk this way...

Artwork by Vernon Morris

Bipedal dinosaurs made the tracks 175 million years ago.

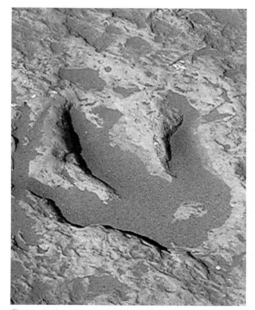

Three-toed tracks are the most abundant.

Dinosaur eggs? Although that's what the guides call it, I have my doubts.

Moenave Petroglyphs

Be sure to ask the guides about the incredible petroglyphs nearby in Moenave, a small settlement just to the north of the dino tracks. If you're lucky they'll take you to them and you'll be witness to one of the finest petroglyph sites in the state. The site is only a 5-minute car ride from the tracks and, like them, are very near the road. But you MUST hire a guide—you are not allowed on the site without one. This spot is still utilized by local native tribes and they may not grant you access if it's during an important ceremonial time. If they do take you, be sure to tip an extra generous amount. If they don't, tough luck—you can't go there unescorted.

The petroglyphs at Moenave may represent clan symbols. They are inscribed on boulders of all sizes.

TURKEY CREEK RUIN

53

Directions:
From Safford, follow Hwy. 70 northwest for 15 miles. Turn west onto Aravaipa-Klondyke Rd. and follow for 32 miles to the town of Klondyke. From Klondyke follow main road north 9 miles to Aravaipa Canyon trailhead. Continue on foot along road. Ruin is a moderate hike of 1⅗ miles up Turkey Creek from parking area.

Contact Info:
BLM Safford Field Office
602-417-9200
www.blm.gov/az/sfo/rec/turkey_creek.htm

Fee:
no fee to visit ruins, but if you are hiking in the nearby Aravaipa Wilderness permits and daily fees are required

Hours: daily

Best time to visit: anytime except in bad weather

Camping/Lodging: basic camping nearby on BLM land

Access:
driving can be very difficult along the dirt road, sometimes requiring 4WD depending on conditions—check in advance before heading out; once there, the hike itself is moderate

Jon's Rating: ★★★½★ (archaeology)
★★★★★ (geology)

Jon's Notes:
Though a rather challenging drive by car, the journey is nonetheless picturesque and the greatest consolation is that the hike isn't bad once you get to the trailhead. IF you get to the trailhead. Turkey Creek ruin is one of the most well-preserved, intact cliff dwellings of the Salado culture and well worth the effort. It appears the site was utilized seasonally from about AD 1300–1450 with the occupants farming and hunting nearby. Please be very careful not to disturb anything as this site is amazingly well-preserved, mostly of its own endurance.

LEFT: It's a bit of a challenge getting here but not too far of a hike once the car is at the trailhead.

TUZIGOOT NATIONAL MONUMENT

54

Directions:
Tuzigoot is about 20 miles west of Sedona. From I-17, take exit #287 and travel west on Hwy. 260 to Cottonwood. In Cottonwood, take Main Street north toward Clarkdale and follow the signs.

Contact Info:
National Park Service
Visitor Information
928-634-5564
www.nps.gov/tuzi

Fee: per person or group entrance fee

Hours: summer: 8am–6pm; winter: 8am–5pm

Best time to visit: anytime; avoid midday heat in summer

Camping/Lodging: camping nearby at Dead Horse Ranch State Park; lodging in Jerome or Cottonwood

Access: easy, paved ⅓-mile loop is a little too steep for wheelchairs

Jon's Rating: ★★★★☆ (archaeology)

Jon's Notes:
Tuzigoot is an ancient pueblo built by the Sinagua culture people. It consisted of 110 rooms including second- and third-story structures. The first buildings were built around AD 1000 and were occupied until about AD 1400. The 42-acre site is situated on a hill overlooking the Verde River and has a commanding view of the valley. The foundations of many of the structures are exposed and the whole area has undergone systematic excavation. Some reconstructed buildings on the site allow you to enter and experience a multi-story pueblo as it may have been a thousand years ago—with forgivable exception of the tall doorways, which was not likely to have been part of the site building code at the time of the Sinagua. The trails are short and easy.

LEFT: Tuzigoot is a group of prehistoric condos offering the finest in amenities.

The Sinagua Culture
picked this hill
near Jerome to
build one of their
finest developments.

Now with Pond Views...

Tuzigoot is perfectly situated atop a small hill that overlooks the Verde Valley and has panoramic views across 360 degrees. When you visit it's easy to see the flat farm fields directly below the hill that were once cultivated by Sinagua peoples 1,000 years ago. It may even look like the cultivation is continuing but it's not, unless you consider toxic runoff from an ore processor something worth harvesting. Sadly, the whole area is dominated by the huge mines near Jerome and these once-farmed fields are evaporation ponds for ore processing plants. But at least they didn't level the hill in the name of progress!

You get a real feeling of Sinagua living on your self-guided tour.

V-BAR-V RANCH

Directions:
From Phoenix, drive north on I-17 to the Sedona interchange exit #298. Follow FR618 east over the Beaver Creek bridge. Soon after the bridge there's a three-way fork in the road with signage leading to V-Bar-V to the right.

Contact Info:
Coconino National Forest/Red Rock Ranger District
928-282-4119
http://en.wikipedia.org/wiki/V-Bar-V_Heritage_Site

Fee:
no fee to enter site but you must have a Red Rock vehicle pass, which you can purchase here

Hours: 9:30am–3:30pm Saturday, Sunday and Monday only

Best time to visit: anytime; avoid midday heat in summer

Camping/Lodging:
none at the park; camping nearby at Beaver Creek; lodging at Sedona

Access: easy, level ¾-mile round-trip dirt trail

Jon's Rating: ★★★★★ (archaeology)

Jon's Notes:
Until recently V-Bar-V Ranch was under private ownership by that rare type of person who actually appreciated the site and preserved its integrity by building a barrier around it and keeping visitation to a minimum. The result is one of the best preserved and least vandalized petroglyph sites in the state. The site itself is fenced and gated so you will need to check in at the small visitor center/museum where the managers—who are always upbeat and friendly—arrange to guide you to the petroglyphs a short distance away. Be prepared to be overwhelmed by the sheer number, variety and quality of petroglyphs—you'll think you're on drugs!

LEFT and RIGHT: One of the best examples of petroglyph sites in the Southwest also happens to be very accessible.

A huge variety of animals, anthropomorphs and geometric symbols are found at the ranch.

What Were They Thinking?

One of the interesting aspects of V-Bar-V is its unlikely location. Most other petroglyph sites are directly associated with permanent waterways, pecked into rocks overlooking a creek or surrounding the edges of a healthy spring. Some are situated high up, atop buttes or cliffs in a spot with sweeping panoramic views. But V-Bar-V is, seemingly, neither. It's nestled in a low area, among a cluster of trees, and quite removed from the nearby river. This could suggest several things: the Indians may have camped near the rock, avoiding the river floodplain for obvious reasons. Or the outcrop may have been situated along ancient trade routes and served as something of a prehistoric billboard to passers-by. Or perhaps it was a sacred site that was visited only on special occasions. Ongoing excavations at the site may reveal more clues to the mystery.

V-Bar-V is in a beautiful setting not far from Sedona.

Directions:
From Page, follow U.S. 89 southwest about 25 miles where it intersects with 89A at the thriving metropolis of Bitter Springs (population 2). Turn right toward Marble Canyon. In about 15 miles, cross over Colorado River at Navajo Bridge and see the start of the cliffs right in front of you.

Contact Info:
Arizona Strip Field Office
435-688-3246
http://arizona.sierraclub.org/monuments/vermilion/vermilion.html

Fee:
you don't need a permit for most of this region but there are some areas—like Paria Canyon—where they are required

Hours: daily

Best time to visit:
anytime; avoid midsummer heat—there's not much shade

Camping/Lodging:
basic camping on the Monument land; lodging in Page

Access: very difficult to extreme

Jon's Rating: ★★★★★ (geology)
★★★½☆ (archaeology)

Jon's Notes:
Wild, remote and difficult to access, the newly created 293,000-acre Vermilion Cliffs National Monument is a spectacular land of arches, amphitheaters, slot canyons, colorful cliffs and awesome vistas. Although it rivals the Grand Canyon in beauty, it is hardly visited due largely to its remote, rugged and sometimes impassable roads. The single exception for pavement-lovers is U.S. Rt. 89A southwest of Page, which crosses the Colorado River at Marble Canyon (it might look like marble to some, but there is no real marble here) and skirts around the south side of the monument along the Vermilion Cliffs on its way to Jacob Lake. Travel this road in the evening and you'll understand how the monument got its name. As with Agua Fria, archaeological sites abound here but you'll need a guide to find any of them. Ask the Chamber of Commerce or outfitters in Page.

LEFT: It's nearly as wonderful as the Grand Canyon but not as easy to get to.

WALNUT CANYON NATIONAL MONUMENT

Directions:
From Flagstaff, head east on I-40 for 7½ miles to exit 204, then south 3 miles to the visitor center.

Contact Info:
Walnut Canyon National Monument Visitor Center
928-526-3367
www.nps.gov/waca

Fee: per person or group entrance fee

Hours: daily 9am–5pm; closed Christmas Day

Best time to visit: anytime; avoid during rain and snow

Camping/Lodging: none at Monument; both nearby in Flagstaff

Access: easy to moderately difficult

Jon's Rating: ★★★★½ (archaeology)
★★★½☆ (geology)

Jon's Notes:
It's bad enough trying to take in all that Flagstaff has to offer without throwing Walnut Canyon into the mix. But if you're not too pressed for time, this easily accessed monument has over 240 ancient Sinagua Indian sites worthy of your admiration. Trails range from the easy, paved Rim Trail, which has great overlooks (bring your binoculars), to the moderately difficult Island Trail, which has 242 steps (there are plenty of rest benches) and passes right by two dozen ruins, some of which you may enter. An informative sign at the top of the steps leading down to the Island Trail declares "Cliff Houses Are Not Toilets!" No wonder there's no rolls of TP in them.

LEFT: Natural overhangs of the Coconino Sandstone make for great patios in the ancient cliff dwellings of Walnut Canyon.

The Island Trail takes you right by dozens of cliff dwellings, some of which you can enter.

Time to Move

Walnut Canyon wasn't always the aristocratic luxury condo community that you see today. Some pit houses in the area above it date from about AD 500, indicating that previous cultures had already settled the region long before the cliff-loving folks came along. Most of these cliff dwellings were constructed around AD 1125 by the Sinagua who lived here for a little over 100 years. By AD 1250 the area was abandoned, possibly as a result of poor soil and failing crops. It is surmised most of the inhabitants moved to Anderson Mesa, a few miles southeast, and set up housekeeping there.

The Sinagua were master ceramic artists fashioning pots both simple and ornate.

WINDOW ROCK

58

Directions:
Located near the New Mexico state line. From I-40, travel north on Reservation Rt. 12 for about 22 miles to Hwy. 264, then east 3 miles to Reservation Rt. 7. Drive north about 1 mile and turn right toward Navajo Tribal Headquarters where you'll find Window Rock itself looming large over you.

Contact Info:
Navajo Nation Parks
928- 871-6647
www.navajonationparks.org

Fee: the park at the base of Window Rock is free

Hours: daylight hours

Best time to visit: anytime

Camping/Lodging: no camping but there is lodging nearby

Access: very easy

Jon's Rating: ★★★☆☆ (geology)
★★★☆☆ (archaeology)

Jon's Notes:
The capital of the Navajo Nation is not in Navajo, it's in Window Rock, Arizona, a good distance away. The "window" itself is stunning. This is a holy place to the Navajo whose primary tribal council head-

quarters is housed in a building facing the sacred site. Please do not walk under the arch as it is considered disrespectful to do so. Also of interest, 1 mile to the south are the "Haystacks"—rounded sandstone monoliths that resemble giant, well, haystacks and is the location of the Navajo Tribal Museum, itself well worth a stop.

LEFT: The "Window" is the political and spiritual center of the Navajo Nation.

WUPATKI NATIONAL MONUMENT

59

Directions:
From Flagstaff, take U.S. 89 north for 26 miles, turn right at sign for Wupatki National Monument. The Visitor Center is 14 miles from this junction and if you stop at all the ruins along the way, it'll probably take you 2–3 hours to reach it.

Contact Info:
National Park Service
Visitor Information
928-679-2365
www.nps.gov/wupa

Fee:
per person entrance fee but your pass also allows you access to Sunset Crater Volcano National Monument to the south

Hours: daily 9am–5pm; may be open longer during summer

Best time to visit: anytime; avoid midday heat in summer

Camping/Lodging:
no camping or lodging within the monument; primitive camping on Coconino Forest lands nearby; closest lodging is Flagstaff

Access: easy to moderate short hikes for all the main ruins

Jon's Rating: ★★★★★ (archaeology)
★★★☆☆ (geology)

Jon's Notes:
On a forbidding windy plano northeast of Flagstaff is a cluster of great archeological sites and you'll wonder why. The place is truly desolate—there's no natural permanent water supply from here to the horizon. But obviously it wasn't always like this, as the 800 ruins and 2,700 archaeological sites attest. Over 800 years ago, several large communities thrived in this region for about a century. Wupatki was a capital and major regional trade center of the Sinagua people between AD 1120–1225. Although most of the monument is off-limits, many of the best sites are open. If you have the time and want a completely unique experience, sign up for the moderate 14-mile hike to Crack-in-the-Rock. This interesting location is named for a narrow crack in the sandstone butte through which one must crawl in order to reach the nicely defensible site. Numerous petroglyphs are found here also.

LEFT: Wupatki was an elaborate multi-story pueblo that invites you into its past.

ABOVE: Just a portion of the main ruins.

RIGHT: The ball court at Wupatki.

But Wait—There's More!

The entrance fee for Wupatki is also honored at Sunset Crater, which is along the southern part of the loop road connecting the two. Although they are not very synonymous in respect to archaeology or geology, each one is interesting in its own way. And being the penny pincher you are, you may as well take advantage of the fact you get two monuments for the price of one. When entering the loop road from the Wupatki side—that is, the north entrance (15 miles from the south)—you will encounter several other ruins in the monument well before Wupatki Ruin itself. They are all worth a stop. Lomaki Pueblo and Box Canyon Dwelling are about 4 miles from the entrance. Both are situated right along the walls of small canyons. In contrast, Nalakihu Pueblo, a short distance away, is built along the slope of a small butte, while Citadel Pueblo rests atop it. Citadel has a very unique and aesthetic architecture that utilizes both red sandstone slabs and black basalt boulders in its walls, an uncommon construction rarely seen. Wukoki Pueblo is east of the Visitor Center about 3½ miles and would be the first ruin you encounter if you have taken the loop from Sunset Crater.

The construction at Wupatki is as precise as any stone masonry built today.

Lomaki and Box Canyon Ruins are very near each other and situated right along-side small canyons.

Nalakihu Pueblo (top) is located at the base of the small butte which holds the aptly-named Citadel Pueblo (bottom).

MUSEUMS

Amerind Foundation
www.amerind.org
2100 N Amerind Rd, Dragoon, AZ 85609
520-586-3666

Founded by industrialist William S. Fulton, Amerind (short for American Indian) is dedicated to collecting and diffusing knowledge about the native cultures of the Southwest. It is primarily an archaeology center with one of the best and most extensive artifact collections in the state.

Arizona Sonora Desert Museum
www.desertmuseum.org
2021 N. Kinney Rd, Tucson, AZ 85743
520-883-2702

An extraordinary blend of nature and science, the Arizona-Sonora Desert Museum is a world-renowned zoo, natural history museum and botanical garden, all in one place. Exhibits re-create the natural landscape of the vast Sonoran Desert Region with 2 miles of pathways traversing 21 acres of beautiful desert.

Arizona State Museum
www.statemuseum.arizona.edu
University of Arizona, 1013 E University Blvd, Tucson, AZ 85721
520-621-6302

At Arizona State Museum you experience the vibrant indigenous cultures of Arizona and northern Mexico through exhibitions, educational programs, a research library and a museum store. The museum's scholars and extensive collections are among the most significant resources in the world for the study of Southwest peoples.

Cave Creek Museum
www.cavecreekmuseum.org
Basin and Skyline, Cave Creek, AZ 85327
480-488-2764

An extensive collection of prehistoric and historic artifacts describe the lives of Indians, miners, ranchers and pioneers.

Chandler Museum

www.chandlermuseum.org

178 E Commonwealth Ave, Chandler, AZ 85225

480-782-2717

The Chandler Museum was established under the Chandler Historical Society in 1969 as a nonprofit organization to preserve the rich history and heritage of Chandler. Although primary focus is on pioneers, there is a great Hohokam Indian presentation as well as other Indian exhibits.

Colorado River Indian Tribes Museum

Rt. 1, Box 23-B, Parker, AZ 85344

928-669-1335

The Colorado River Indian Tribes Museum and Library features the Mohave, Chemehuevi, Navajo and Hopi Indian Tribes. You will learn about these tribes past and present. The museum has an extensive collection of locally made Indian crafts.

Graham County Historical Society

www.rootsweb.com/~azgraham/museum.html

3430 W Hwy. 70, Thatcher, AZ 85546

520-348-0069

The museum contains general historic displays on Graham County with rooms set aside for prehistory, saddles, military, kitchen, bedroom and parlor displays in addition to many topical displays to be found in the main museum room. Many of the topical displays in the main room rotate periodically. The museum also houses a modest library of pertinent books plus an extensive collection of printed materials in vertical files.

Heard Museum

www.heard.org

2301 N Central, Phoenix, AZ 85004

602-252-8848

The mission and philosophy of the Heard Museum today is to educate the public about the heritage and the living cultures and arts of Native peoples, with an emphasis on the peoples of the Southwest. It is one of the best Southwestern-cultures-oriented museums in the U.S.

Mesa Southwest Museum

www.mesasouthwestmuseum.com
53 N Macdonald, Mesa, Az 85201
480-644-2230

The Mesa Southwest Museum is Arizona's premier museum of cultural and natural history, exploring the Southwest's history from the time before the dinosaurs to the present day.

Museum of Anthropology

www.azcama.com/museums/asu_anthro_museum.htm
Located at Arizona State University, Tempe, AZ
480-965-6213

The purpose of the ASU Museum of Anthropology is to preserve, interpret, display and study anthropological material from the subdisciplines of archaeology, physical archaeology, physical anthropology and socio-cultural anthropology.

Museum of Northern Arizona

www.musnaz.org
3101 N Ft. Valley Rd, Flagstaff, AZ 86001
928-774-5213

This excellent facility is located in the pine hills of Flagstaff. Their mission is to "inspire a sense of love and responsibility for the beauty and diversity of the Colorado Plateau through collecting, studying, interpreting, and preserving the region's natural and cultural heritage." This about says it all, except that it's one of the best museums in the state.

Navajo Nation Museum

www.navajo.org
Hwy. 264 & Post Office Loop Rd, Window Rock, AZ 86515
928-871-7941

The modern Navajo Museum is dedicated to preserving and interpreting the rich and unique culture of the Navajo Nation. Native displays, a book and gift shop, snack bar, auditorium, outdoor amphitheater, information kiosk, library and on-site authentic Navajo hogan complete the center.

Rim Country Museum

www.rimcountrymuseums.com

700 Green Valley Pkwy., Payson, AZ 85547

928-474-3483

This museum opens with an exhibit introducing you to the world of the archaeologist. From there you are guided through by text and exhibits by Ao Ao, one of the elders of their "Ancient Culture" who lived around 1200 AD.

Smoki Museum

www.smokimuseum.org

147 N Arizona, Prescott, AZ 86304

928-445-1230

Designed to resemble an Indian pueblo, the Smoki Museum was built in 1935 of native stone and wood. It was constructed with labor provided by the Civilian Works Administration and the Smoki People. The Smoki People were a group of Prescott citizens organized in 1921 and dedicated to the perpetuation of American Indian ceremonies and dances, which they do quite well in this forum.

Tempe Historical Society

www.tempe.gov/museum/emuseum.htm

809 E Southern Ave, Tempe, AZ 85282

480-350-5100

The Tempe Historical Museum is a center where the community comes together to celebrate Tempe's past and ponder the future. Permanent and changing exhibits, educational programs and research projects generally focus on some aspect of Tempe's history within the context of state and national events.

Willow Bend Environmental Education Center

www.edu-source.com

703 E Sawmill Rd, Flagstaff, AZ 86001

928-779-1745

This interesting facility is sponsored by the Coconino and Fredonia Natural Resource Conservation Districts. It is essentially a natural history and environmental learning center. There are hands-on exhibits in a straw-bale building.

REFERENCES AND WEBSITES

References

Bostwick, Todd W. *Landscape of the Spirits.* Tucson, AZ: University of Arizona Press, 2002.

Chronic, Halka. *Roadside Geology of Arizona.* Missoula, MT: Mountain Press Publishing, 1989.

Cunkle, James R. and Markus A. Jacquemain. *Stone Magic of the Ancients.* Phoenix, AZ: Golden West Publishers, 1996.

Ferguson, William M. and Arthur H. Rohn. *Anasazi Ruins of the Southwest in Color.* Albuquerque, NM: University of New Mexico Press, 1990.

Noble, David Grant. *Ancient Ruins of the Southwest.* Flagstaff, AZ: Northland Publishing, 2000.

Malotki, Ekkehart and Donald E. Weaver. *Stone Chisel and Yucca Brush.* Walnut, CA: Kiva Publishing, 2002.

McCreery, Patricia and Ekkehart Malotki. *Tapamveni.* Petrified Forest, AZ: Petrified Forest Museum Association, 1994.

Reid, Jefferson and Stephanie Whittlesey. *The Archaeology of Ancient Arizona.* Tucson, AZ: University of Arizona Press, 1997.

Websites

Government websites:
www.nps.gov
www.pr.state.az.us
www.fs.fed.us
www.az.blm.gov

Other non-commercial websites:
www.azmuseums.org
www.centerfordesertarchaeology.org
www.americansouthwest.net/arizona

Commercial websites:
http://rockart.esmartweb.com
www.sidecanyon.com
www.hikearizona.com

GLOSSARY

anthropomorph OK I admit this sounds a bit out there but here goes: Anthropomorphs are rock art images which resemble human forms, at least a little. Some folks think they're more likely space aliens which could account for the many strange appendages and ornamentations often found within these images. Not to mention the sudden disappearance of guidebook authors at such sites.

archaeology Why are you asking me this? You should know it already! It's basically the study of ancient cultures, their remains, artifacts, structures, and influences.

Archaic In North America, the native cultures which predate the ancestral pueblo peoples (Hisatsinom) but occur after Clovis time. The Archaic period is roughly defined as running from about 6,000 BC to about 900 BC.

basalt It's old lava—simple as that.

Clovis Primarily refers to a distinct form of stone tool manufacturing. Clovis points are fundamentally more refined and advanced than previously fabricated tools. The term also, more loosely, defines cultures that fall within a temporal context after PaleoIndians but predating Archaic. Generally considered from about 10,000–6,000 years BC.

desert patina/desert varnish The effect is as if some cosmic woodworker spilled a very large bucket of dark stain over the desert floor, coating all the exposed rock on the surface. That stain is comprised mostly of iron oxides that color the outer surface dark brown to black, while the inside is the natural rock color, usually much lighter.

differential weathering See "selective weathering".

eye Here I take the easy way out and pull that old dictionary trick by telling you to go look up the term "window" which, lucky for you, actually is defined on page 267.

finder's fee A catchy term we use to make you feel like you owe us some percentage of profits that you may realize from your hard work and ingenuity inspired by reading this book. Send us a check and we'll call it even.

geoglyph A singularly cool archeological site made by aligning/piling rocks into designs and shapes, or, alternatively, by deliberate removal of stones from an area creating recognizable patterns in the ground.

geology A very cool and hip career if you can make a living at it, which most geology graduates have a hard time doing. The term refers to the study of the Earth and the processes that continue to shape it.

Hephaestus The ancient Greek god of fire, son of Zeus and Hera. Probably not someone you'd want to get mad at you.

Hisatsinom A somewhat loosely-defined group which primarily refers to ancestral Hopi. The Hisatsinom had their start as a recognizable group about 900 BC, just after the Archaic.

lava You should know this already, but here's a little more info for ya: Yes, we all know this is volcanic in origin. But lava need not have come from a stereotypical volcano. It often arrives by out-pouring from large cracks in the Earth's crust.

lava tube A natural tunnel that forms when a lava 'river' exits from a channel in the lava flow.

lithology Refers to rock—and I don't mean rock-and-roll bands. Rather it's all about stony rock—the different types, their composition, and the processes that produce them. Also can mean the subdivision of geology which studies rock.

magma Molten rock or lava before it has cooled.

metate Stone grinding surface used by native cultures to pulverize corn and other plant material.

PaleoIndian Term given to all ancestral Indians that predate well-documented dominant native cultures. In North America this generally refers to any pre-Clovis peoples older than about 8,000 years.

paleontology The study of fossils, which, in turn, has nothing to do with the watch-making company of the same name.

petroglyph Petro means rock, glyph means form. Can you add them and come up with something other than "rock form"? This term also references the way in which the image is made—etched or inscribed into the rock face by pecking away the outer surface.

pictograph Meaningful painting on rocks by ancient cultures. (As opposed to meaningless painting on subway cars, which we scientists call "graffiti".)

pueblo Do I really need to spell this out for you? OK, it's a term used to denote a communal building structure that generally houses multiple families and is the center of activity for a given community.

rhyolite/rhyolitic tuff A loose term which describes an equally loose-cemented extrusive volcanic rock. Rhyolites form in similar fashion to basalts but are usually much softer and more easily eroded.

riparian Has nothing to do with repairing anything. Refers to natural environments that abide along permanent waterways. Home to wildlife galore.

selective weathering/selective erosion The key here is "selective"—like "selective service" when Uncle Sam calls you up for military duty and doesn't call up your pot-head neighbor. Certain rocks are softer than others and erode away much faster, leaving the harder, more durable, rock to stand out like a Marine Special Forces recruit in a monastery.

sink If you're thinking of the catchment basins in your house then you're not too far off. Now imagine a depression in the ground which effectively performs similarly to your kitchen sink and you've got it.

tree-ring dating You're probably astute enough to know this phrase isn't hinting at a romantic night out between two annular growths of tall woody plants. But what you may not know is it refers to an absolute method of dating ruins which contain preserved tree parts in their structure. By looking at the patterns in the annular rings, researchers are often able to match them precisely with known records of tree growth, thereby pinpointing the years the tree was alive.

volcanic bomb It's not something likely to turn up in Transportation Safety Administration (TSA) checks of luggage at the airports, but you never know. When a volcano explodes and hurls liquid magma skyward, the globs cool and harden as they fly through the air, developing tell-tale shapes before hitting the ground or clueless bystanders.

window If you had a solid wall on your house that you wanted to let the sun shine through, what would you do? Smash a hole in the sucker, of course. That bit of handiwork is called a window. Now let me ask you—why should Mother Nature shy away from doing the same thing when she wants to have sunlight stream through a hard rock wall?

INDEX

ABOUT THE AUTHORS

Jon Kramer is an adventurer first, and also a geologist, writer, climber and surfer (but not necessarily in that order, depending on the surf). He received his Bachelor of Science degree in geology at the University of Maryland and has pursued life as an adventuring paleontologist ever since. His interests are quite varied and include all things natural. In addition to popular travel and adventure writing, Jon has published scientific papers on critters as ancient as 2 billion-year-old bacteria and as young as 12,000-year-old mammoths. Jon travels extensively with his wife Julie, sometimes settling down for a rest in Minnesota, Florida, California and interesting points in between.

Julie Martinez is an explorer, naturalist, freelance artist and formal art instructor. Her appreciation for insects, plants, rocks and fossils started in childhood with a collection that has grown throughout her life. Julie graduated from the University of Wisconsin, Stevens Point, with a degree in Fine Arts and Biology. She initially worked as an illustrator for the medical field but in the late 1980s began a freelance career, which she has enjoyed ever since. Julie's work is featured in many textbooks, journals and museum exhibits throughout North America. She is also a staff teacher at Minnesota School of Botanical Art. When not teaching, she travels with Jon, exploring the wilds of the world.

Vernon Morris is a freelance artist, muralist and adventuring time traveler. His formal art education took place in the early 1980s at the University of Minnesota and Minneapolis College of Art and Design. Vern's Native American (Anishinabe) roots have been a powerful influence in his life. He maintains a small quarry at Pipestone National Monument where he excavates the famous carving stone every year. He then sculpts it into pipes and ritual objects just as his ancestors did for countless generations. Vern carries his work with him into the wilds and is just as comfortable carving pipestone atop a mesa in the Southwest as sketching scenes from antiquity along the ocean in Big Sur.

NOTES

NOTES

NOTES

NOTES